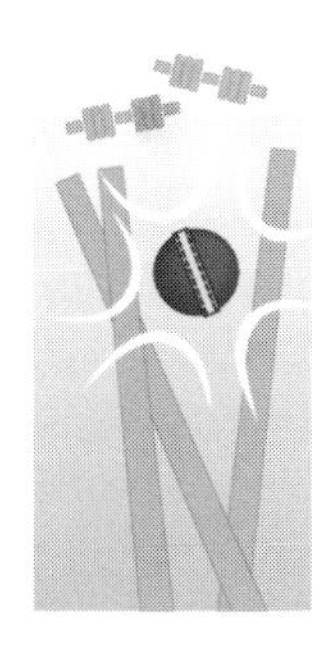

GOING BATS IN NORFOLK

For family and friends who share my timeless views on the boundary's edge...

"His memories arose in multitude as he sat composedly there, cricket coincidences, humours, personal touches among them but not only those; for he had discerned that the game itself, if it is found in its natural bearings, is only the agreeable wicket-gate to a landscape of human joys and sorrows, and is greatest where it fades away most imperceptibly into their wider horizon."

Edmund Blunden, Cricket Country

GOING BATS IN NORFOLK

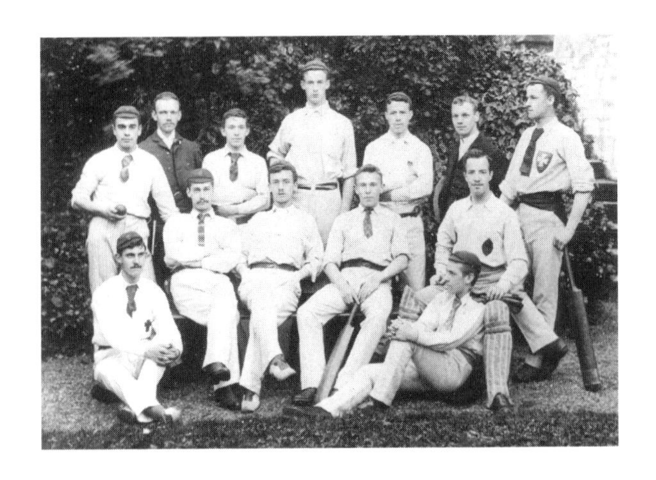

True cricketing tales from Keith Skipper

"The Boy from Cowpat Corner"

HALSGROVE

First published in Great Britain in 2010

Title page: *Mileham and Lexham line-up in the early 1900s.*

British Library Cataloguing-in-Publication Data
A CIP record for this title is available from the British Library

ISBN 978 0 85704 074 9

HALSGROVE
Halsgrove House,
Ryelands Industrial Estate,
Bagley Road, Wellington, Somerset TA21 9PZ
Tel: 01823 653777 Fax: 01823 216796
email: sales@halsgrove.com

Part of the Halsgrove group of companies
Information on all Halsgrove titles is available at: www.halsgrove.com

Printed and bound by SRP Ltd., Exeter

Bradfield players and officials (note the natty headgear) line up in the 1940s.

BATTING ORDER

Acknowledgements

I am grateful to a host of local enthusiasts for helping me pay tribute to the best game in an ideal setting. My four brothers, Maurice, Malcolm, Colin and Mick, formed a telling team of village raconteurs with sharp memories for statistics.

Norfolk, with an occasional leg glance towards old friends in Suffolk, provides true inspiration from Cowpat Corner to County Headquarters.

Special thanks to Tom Walshe and Derek Moore as they built fascinating chapters around their own club adventures. Rich character sketches underline the depth of friendship and fun on offer to those wishing to share.

Philip Yaxley, such a valued collector of precious images to illustrate our scorebooks of history, leads a grand parade of pictorial supporters.

Rest of the roll call sounds like a handy touring party for a series of village contests punctuated by pub intermissions. I'm in the chair, so its halves of mild and packets of coypu-flavoured crisps for: Derek Bales, Gordon Chivers, Mike Davage, Mike Farman, Ray Fenn, Frank Gordon, David Gregson, Tim Knight, Douglas and Bob Millar, Pat Newman, Richard Shepheard, Mike Staines, Chris Sugden, David Turner, Leslie Ward, Roger Wilson, Maurice Woods and David Woodward.

For all others who have kept me awake, entertained and informed over the seasons, a promise not to mention again a certain hat-trick I claimed against a club destined for the top.

For my sons Danny and Robin, eternal gratitude for not sniggering out loud when they saw me play. They knew it was different in the good old days.

For my wife Diane, another heartfelt burst of applause for keeping me in the team at Caister with her stunning strawberry flans for the tea interval.

Keith Skipper,
Cromer, 2010

Players, spectators and scorers on the boundary as Rackheath go into action at The Grange in the 1950s.

BITTER SWEET

King Willow now doth make his bow;
His glories I acclaim,
Some call him slow, which may be so,
Some say that he is tame.
But when the ground is nearly drowned –
Each May it is the same –
You must agree cricket to be
A most abandoned game!

How sweet in May to see the way
The slips freeze in the blast,
While cover-point feels every joint
Refrigerating fast!
How sweetly blows the umpire's nose
When skies are overcast,
Turning instead of pink and red
To pretty blue at last!

How sweet to bat while pit-a-pat
The rain begins to spout!
How sweet to get your feet as wet
As fins beneath a trout!
How sweet to slide and hurt your side!
How sweet, beyond all doubt,
When once the pav, you entered have,
To find the fire's not out!

King Willow now doth make his bow;
His glories I extol.
Give me a day in drenching May,
Give me a ball to bowl,
Give me a pitch, I'll count me rich,
And you can have the whole
Terrestrial earth for what it's worth,
Including the North Pole!

Herbert Farjeon

ONE

MODESTY MAY

The gorse is ablaze. Bluebells are congregating in secret places. Rogue lupins will soon be on the march alongside heavy traffic. Rain stops play now and again.

A fresh cricket season, with so many impatient batsmen trying to blast and clout before May is out. The more temperate see regular double figures by the end of the month as a reasonable target.

Neville Cardus, who wrote majestically about a game that has inspired more literary innings than any other, pointed out many blossom-shakers ago: "A season does not burst on us, as football does, full grown and arrogant.

"It comes to us every year with a modesty that matches the slender tracery of leaf and twig, which belongs to the setting of every true cricket field in the season's first days."

Cricket has drawn to it enough of the right sort of people throughout its history, possibly in readiness to cope with little difficulties like Bodyline, Kerry Packer, arguments with umpires, ball tampering and pyjama games.

The first-class scene has stolen from the village green to revive its financial fortunes and attract new interest. Purists still frown on the one-day and limited over carnivals as they fill grounds all over the world.

William Blake wrote a poem about the game. Lord Byron played for Harrow. James Joyce was an enthusiast. Samuel Beckett is the only Nobel Prize-winner for Literature to have appeared in Wisden.

Many other academics and literary figures like Edmund Blunden, R C Sherriff, Siegfried Sassoon and Hugh de Selincourt took cricket as a diversion, albeit one to be passionately admired.

Then there was J M Barrie, biggest inspiration for those of us for whom skill has never been able to match enthusiasm. The creator of Peter Pan didn't want to grow up and his love affair with cricket never waned.

He formed a team of literary colleagues who were also fond of the game but, to put it mildly, short on talent. Barrie led them frequently to resounding defeat. The more distinguished as authors were his men, the worse they played – with the notable exception of Conan Doyle.

On the train journey to their first match, Barrie tried to get across finer points of the game. Like which side of the bat you hit with. He asked two African travellers the African for "Heaven help us!" The reply was " Allahakbar", and from this the side took the name The Allahakbarries.

Plenty of jokes followed that neat pun and Barrie excelled himself in a booklet presented to each member of the team. Let me suggest every local club skipper prepares a similar feast as a new campaign beckons:

"Watson – an invaluable man in the train going down. Very safe bat in the train. Loses confidence when told to go in.

"Whibley – hits blooming hard, blooming high – and blooming seldom.

"Ford – nicknamed 'Lost-ball Ford' because he and the ball are seldom in the same field.

"Frederic – worst batsman in the world. Equally at home with the ball."

Self-deprecating humour also ran through a list of useful hints from the thoughtful captain:

"Should you hit the ball, run at once. Don't stop to cheer.

"If bowled first ball, pretend that you only came out for the fun of the thing. Then go away and sit by yourself behind the hedge.

"Don't practise on opponents' grounds before match begins. This can only give them confidence."

Vibrant proof that cricket not only attracts performers of modest ability; it does its level best to accommodate them. I benefitted from that charitable streak for nearly as many summers as I scored runs, took wickets or held catches.

Of course, a few unfortunate souls will never understand the game. Abdul Aziz, also known as Abdul the Damned, was a Turkish potentate who, on seeing English sailors plays cricket, exclaimed: "Remarkable! But what needless exertion! Why do you not compel your slaves and concubines to perform it for you?"

Some adopt a rather snobbish and dismissive stance. Like George Bernard Shaw. On being told England had been successful in the Australian Tests, he asked what they had been testing.

Rudyard Kipling said cricket was "casting a ball at three straight sticks and defending the same with a fourth." Poetic turn of phrase.

Yes, cricket has been known to prompt over-the-top reaction. Dr Heath, headmaster at Eton, was a perfectionist. He flogged the school XI – and the poor little wing-collared scorer –when they returned from a defeat by Westminster School.

For the bulk of the game's ardent admirers, however, it is easy to keep a sense of proportion. Take this item from the personal column of

World Sport as a good example;

"Retired gentleman wishes to meet widow with two tickets for the Third Test with view to matrimony. Kindly send photographs of tickets."

Odd statistics, personality pieces, chuckles at somebody else's expense. All part of a summer canvas as cricket continues to suggest a tranquil and unchanging order in an age of bewildering flux.

Perfect delivery from Neville Cardus; "I should challenge the Englishness of any man who could walk down a country lane, come unexpectedly on a cricket match and not lean over the fence and watch for a while."

Especially if The Allahakbarries are in action, pitting their inestimable skills against a Norfolk village team while dragonflies play hide-and-seek among the thistle-down and a magpie flaps lazily across the meadow.

Enough to lure John Arlott back to the microphone to sigh; "England, their England..."

TESTING TEAM

Norfolk's cricket authorities have scanned the county and contacted the England Test selectors with an offer of "a home-grown village team capable of at least stretching the Aussies".

It reads; Bale, Bylaugh, Clippesby, Edgefield, Overstrand, Outwell, Runhall, Testerton, Three Holes (Capt.), Pulham Market and Swardeston. Umpires; Len Wade and Stan Hoe.

TWO

VILLAGE ROOTS

Cowpat Corner sticks in my memory as the ideal spot from which to launch a glittering career. But I didn't want to be a budding botanist, butterfly collector, bug spotter or bovine expert.

For those unfamiliar with pastoral cricket settings but a few gentle overs ago, let me emphasise just how gloriously rough and unready some of them could be.

Manicured playing fields, lovingly-prepared pitches, freshly-painted pavilions and healthy social clubs were mirages way beyond the village duck pond as a benevolent local farmer invited devotees of the great summer game, some of them in his employ, to share a meadow with his herd of dairy cattle or frisky bullocks.

Electric fencing went up around the sacred square to prevent too

Dick Hammond leads the Beeston team a few seasons before the author began his scoring career.

much impromptu watering or heavy manuring before the next fixture. Inquisitive animals were marched off to alternative pastures while sport commandeered their country stage.

Playing surfaces were often unpredictable and sides batting first didn't give up hope just because they'd been shot out for fewer than 50. "That's a decent score on here" was no idle boast on certain grounds where buttercups, dandelions, hemlock and mole-hills decorated the picture.

Changing facilities were Spartan to say the least. A shepherd's hut on wheels or an old garden shed on borrowed time might earn "luxury" votes as most players turned up dressed for action or slipped quietly behind the hedge to transform from cowman in overalls into Superman in whites. (Perhaps that should be Batman for those who wielded the willow).

Tea intervals, just like fourses breaks in the harvest field, turned into testing exercises in keeping sandwiches and insects apart as the female army arrived with tasty and moral sustenance. A few clubs put on an indoor spread if village hall or pub were nearby.

Cowpat Corner? That's where many a young hopeful first felt that magic tingle of acceptance into the village sporting hierarchy, a few steps up from becoming milk monitor at school or taking the collection at Chapel. Time and space to weigh it all up out there, to taste the heady cocktail of fear and excitement, to wait for a sure sign that the cricketing gods might be on your side.

To be honest, I always felt slightly confused when sent to patrol an outer territory littered with strange bumps, rabbit holes and cattle calling-cards at third man, fine leg or long-stop directly behind the wicket-keeper. Was I here through the captain's faith in my blossoming athletic prowess... or could it be but a flimsy attempt to hide me as far away from the serious action as possible?

An embarrassing escapade on a baking hot Saturday afternoon in the 1950s when the ball seemed intent on following me for about five deliveries in every over may hold part of the answer.

I had organised several search parties in nettles and brambles beyond the boundary as a whirlwind visiting batsman carved and sliced a succession of fast but short deliveries over the cordon of exasperated slips. I was moved to deep square-leg to catch my breath.

The batsman immediately changed tack to produce an impressive hook shot in my direction. I scuttled backwards as the ball soared towards a blinding sun and returned to Norfolk earth with a resounding squelch. It had zoomed in on a fairly fresh cowpat inches from thick vegetation marking the boundary's edge.

I faced an obvious dilemma as my right plimsoll, specially whitened like the other for the occasion, sank slowly below a crusty surface to retrieve the imprisoned sphere. Should I kick it through the thistles and over the line and signal four or clean it up with some dock leaves and whistle it back into the 'keeper's gloves?

Waiting for playtime... Skipper brothers at their village school. Left to right - Malcolm, Maurice and Keith

I settled for the honest path only to become sadly unstuck. The slippery ball twice went off at crazy tangents. Chortling batsmen mustered enough composure and energy to run six before it was gingerly relayed home. Ironic applause in my direction hinted at a lengthy inquest to dominate the tea break.

Cowpat Corner could follow you around. They'd probably call it something clever like "a sharp learning curve" these days, but I prefer to remember it as a colourful if tricky introduction to a sporting arena springing from deep countryside roots. Some of them still clearly visible.

This is my cricket reverie based on a lifelong passion for the game nurtured through a proud family innings with our village club at Beeston in the middle of the county.

Nearly half-a-century out in the middle as journalist and broadcaster on native soil allowed me to build on a truly modest playing career – "highly extinguished" according to one uncharitable contemporary – with opportunities to spotlight memorable matches, charismatic characters as well as to fall under the spell of delectable settings right across the area.

I could also peep over the wall into a riveting past on discovering articles and books dedicated to outstanding chapters in local sporting history. Like an unofficial Test match at Old Buckenham and a Victorian superstar from Horningtoft.

Throughout the 1970s I lived next door to the Lakenham county ground, a wonderful green lung in the middle of Norwich, and so could glance out of my bedroom window to check on playing progress or see who was first in the queue for the beer tent when rain swept in.

✧✧✧

Caister Cricket Club, a few breezes from the fleshpots of Great Yarmouth, tolerated my inclusion as a trying performer from the mid-1960s for far too many summers of under-achieving. One captain hinted I was selected only for my banter and timeless repartee, but I did get lumbered with the role of serial speechmaker for the annual dinner. I exacted ample one-night revenge for season-long ribbing.

This led to countless free meals and unbridled revelry with mardling on the side at friendly fixtures across the county and occasionally beyond. I took Norfolk humour to Spalding – and got away with it – although social dates in Suffolk usually warranted an interpreter and bodyguard.

I was privileged to be invited to propose toasts at the centenary dinners of Cromer and Bradfield Cricket Clubs, and the Mid-Norfolk Sunday League (close to my roots), whose milestone was marked by a special game at Lakenham in September, 1998.

The second oldest league in the country celebrated in style. Former Lancashire and England batsman Graeme "Foxy" Fowler replied to my toast. Well, only fair ... his home county boasts the oldest league.

The 40th anniversary salute to the Bob Carter Cup knockout competition in April, 2008, gave me another chance to roll back the seasons and exclaim "I was there with notebook in hand" when Dereham beat Hunstanton in the first final.

I have shared the Norfolk club dinner platform with many sporting legends, but perhaps the pick of a star-studded crop arrived at North Runcton in October, 1984. Main speaker was former Surry and England spinner Jim Laker, then a member of the BBC Television cricket commentary team.

He posted remarkable match figures of 19 wickets for 90 runs against the Australians at Old Trafford in 1956. I asked what he said to Surrey colleague Tony Lock for taking the other wicket and so ruining his chances of a clean sweep. Jim smiled and reminded me that personal glory lagged well behind collective satisfaction in victory over the old enemy.

I applaud all those who have kept me company on and off the field since Cowpat Corner first called. Warmest thanks to fellow enthusiasts, invariably more talented than me, for cramming into this little pavilion to share golden memories and reaffirm unswerving commitment to the local cause.

I have enjoyed a grand knock as scorer, umpire, scribe, player (from boy called up in an emergency to captain as a tribute to turning up regularly), groundsman (pitch marker and boundary flag inserter), commentator (mostly on my bike as John Arlott), summariser (for BBC Radio Norfolk at county games), post-match entertainer (Singing Postman numbers a speciality) and best cadger of free lifts on the Norfolk circuit.

Time now to find a comfortable seat at the boundary's edge for a balmy evening of reflection, with the odd pint of bitter and useful rations of banter to fill in gaps between overs. I can also deny persistent rumours that I had a starring role in one of my favourite cricket yarns.

They were a man short at a village match in Norfolk. An enthusiastic spectator was enlisted to make up the numbers. He was sent out to long-on and as the field was on a slope, he was out of sight of the pitch.

Apart from throwing the ball in occasionally, he didn't have much to do. Then a towering hit was sent in his direction. He caught the ball and scampered up the hill shouting; "I caught it! I caught it!".

The batsman glared angrily at him.

"You sorft tewl!" he screamed. "They wuz out 15 minutes ago. We're battin' now!"

HANDY IDEA

Charity matches often introduce a rule forcing batsmen to retire when they reach a certain score, perhaps 50, to stop one player dominating an innings. But a game between veteran Norfolk and Suffolk players at Yarmouth in August, 1906, had a better idea.

If a batsman reached 20 he was forced to continue with his unorthodox hand. A right-handed bat, therefore, would switch to left-handed on reaching the magic number.

This was the second annual match played in aid of Yarmouth Boys' Home and Gorleston Cottage Hospital. The players, aged from 55 to 75, all wore top hats and dress coats to accord with ancient cricket fashions. The bowling was underarm, closely scrutinised by two umpires, both 86 years old.

Mr Papworth's team batted first and were soon in trouble. With the score on 19, Mr Brasnett, the opposing captain, performed the hat-trick, capturing the wickets of Lindsay (stumped), Blanchflower (bowled) and Still (bowled)

Any old-timers wilting in the field were much cheered by the thought that game might soon be over. Fielding was the weak spot. Lacks of mobility meant only two catches were held all day.

Mr Papworth himself was out for eight (35 for 6) but Thompson and Bond put together the best partnership of the match and both were forced to switch hands. An interruption for rain and a good last-wicket stand extended the innings, which closed at 112.

Reverend Pratt gave the Brasnett team a good start until he was forced to switch hands and the captain put on 13 (all singles) with Swindell. When Brasnett was out (62 for 4) a collapse set in and the team were soon all out for 77.

Mr Papworth's team won by 35 runs.

THE CRICKET MATCH

Now we often play cricket on our huntin' ground,
The lads from the village they like ter come down,
From their occupations they come jist ter play,
They'd rather play cricket than sleep in the hay.

Then one day we started, the match wuz begun,
But the Farmer wuz bowled out for one poultry run,
On came the next man; his fust name wuz Fred,
Now he wuz a Blacksmith so he forged ahead.

So we orl play cricket from mornin' ter night
Jist ter prove that our flannels are lovely an' white.

So orl day we batted an' orl day we scored,
Even the Teacher put runs on the board,
Then the old Fam'ly Doctor he knocked up some more,
Symptoms a six an' symptoms a four.

Then orl of a sudden we ran out o' luck,
When the poor ole Poacher wuz caught for a duck,
Then up jumped the Plumber, yew'll never guess what...
When he went ter the wicket his bat he forgot.

So we orl play cricket orl day in the sun,
Jist ter prove that the summer has really begun.

Well our innin's wuz ended, their fust man went in,
But our fieldin' Chemist he dispensed with him,
Then said the Cobbler, a bowler so fast,
"Yew hed the fust man, now I'll hev the last."

Behind the wicket wuz Bookmaker Brown,
He took another with a bob up an' down,
It was left to the Vicar to wind up the match,
When he on the boundary converted a catch.

So we orl play cricket both ole man an' boy
To prove that our cricket we really enjoy.

So now I hev told yew jist how we hev won
With our game of cricket we also hev fun
So go warn the Landlord ter stand by the pumps,
While I tell the Dentist ter pull out the stumps.

So we orl play cricket now let's hev some beer
Jist ter prove that the summer has really bin here.

Allan Smethurst, The Singing Postman

READY FOR ACTION

An amusing incident from a friendly encounter during the Second World War was recalled by David Woodard. He was a pupil at Sir John Leman School in Beccles at the time.

"Games master Pop Glover organised matches between sides made up of staff members, older boys and one or two locals to play against service teams. On one occasion, a local searchlight and ack-ack battery turned up with a motley crew.

"The officer in charge and one or two others arrived with whites, cricket boots and all the gear required. But to make up their side they had recruited some Tommies who had never played in an organised game before.

"Pop offered our visitors use of the school equipment and agreed they could play in khaki trousers if they lacked flannels. There was some delay before their wicket-keeper appeared. Alas, he had adorned himself with an abdominal protector and box, not beneath his khaki uniform but strapped outside like a codpiece!

"A hush round the ground was broken only by the stifled mirth of schoolboy onlookers. The officer in charge quietly led the wicket-keeper back to the dressing-room. He reappeared a few minutes later more suitably attired."

Stanfield and Mileham ready for action in 1920.

Shipdham Cricket Club a few summer's ago.

THREE

KNOW THE SCORE

As one of a family of 10, five boys and five girls, it wasn't hard to think in terms of a cricket team. Especially if Dad could be persuaded to play while Mum did the teas.

Perhaps other big broods in our village of Beeston, mainly going about its farming business in the middle of Norfolk, entertained similar sporting ambitions as community life was stitched back together after the Second World War.

We had an aerodrome as a reminder of how young Americans had come and gone down the cruel runway of fate. A Nissen hut was transformed into our entertainment centre for film shows, dances, whist drives and other social gatherings. A cricket pitch not far from the war memorial told us friendly hostilities had resumed against dastardly crews from the likes of Longham and Wendling.

Crackling commentaries on the old wireless as mighty Bradman held sway for the all-conquering 1948 Australians are among my earliest domestic souvenirs. Dad demanded hush at the tea table or else another little innings down the yard or among the orchard apple trees would be ruled out by "bedtime stops play" notices.

A few seasons later, when summer curfews could stretch as far as seven o'clock, we found scope for proper Test Matches as my mate Michael Rye agreed to let everyone have a turn with his real bat, the only one in the immediate neighbourhood.

With his birthday falling on Christmas Day, Michael, affectionately known as Tubby when he filled out, could combine two special occasions for a "big present". I remember how we created a makeshift pitch in the middle of a meadow covered in ice and snow to give that new bat a proper christening in late December. His real leather football also won a host of admirers and he played the game by not always insisting on going in goal.

Keith with Michael Rye - waiting for the next Test Match

Chapel on a sunswept Sunday afternoon taught me the meaning of eternity as travelling preachers mocked burning desires to catch up with fresh dramas on the cricket meadow. Tidy pencil work had earned me the post of Saturday scorer with its thrilling but scary possibility of being asked to fill a gap in the team when farm duties claimed one of the regulars, especially at harvest time.

I took my trusty pencil to Chapel and tried to while away long and boring sermons by inventing a highly complicated game you could play by yourself based on cricket and the Methodist hymn book. It culminated in those most prolific of hymn writers, brothers Charles and John Wesley, sharing the new ball attack against the rest.

I never completed a fixture during one sermon because there were too many arguments over which end Charles Wesley should take after a lunch of loaves and fishes.

May was the cruellest month for a cricket lover chained to a pew as early-season averages cried out for attention and cup contests still carried genuine hopes of progress. The weather wore its friendliest smile, a mere breeze tickling blossom into confetti showers over green-framed lanes under vivid blue skies.

Now and again I was moved to pray for rain when the fates threw up a Sunday clash with dastardly local rivals, Longham. A delay would mean a mid-week rescheduling and a chance for me to preach my usual propaganda about laws of averages pointing to an overdue Beeston success.

While I was but a shadowy figure on the fringes of Sunday action, an official Saturday job as village scorer, home and away, soon afforded me special status among the grown-ups discussing tactics, enjoying tasty teas and travelling to parts of the Norfolk empire where my bike had yet to venture.

I recall Beeston troops assembling outside the shop near the school to wait for Ralph Cross at the wheel of our team coach – his lorry. After the odd diversion to collect stragglers from an outlying farm or local pubs, The Ploughshare and The Bell, we made ourselves comfortable in the back and headed for the wilds of Tittleshall, Gateley, Rougham, Ryburgh....

Beeston scorer at 11 years old

I often had our transport of delight entirely to myself as darkness crept up after combat. I could hear them laughing and singing in the pub, Albert Hudson claiming his usual starring role as warbler-in-chief, while my rations of Vimto and crisps rapidly dwindled.

Sometimes following an unexpected victory, celebrations could meander towards closing time – and I was the only one to be scolded for being late home! Still, a price worth paying to watch my heroes fall on to the back of the lorry, giggling, shuffling, gesturing, waving to passers-by and playing the game all over again.

Those local derbies against next-door Longham too often ended in Beeston defeat, although I maintained throughout my seasons with the scorebook that we would have enjoyed a better share of cup progress if our most challenging of rivals had shown more respect for the true spirit of the game.

They drafted in "guest" players from Dereham for some mid-week knockout cup matches... within the rules but, to my young mind, hardly in keeping with the aims of peaceful co-existence in this small corner of the county.

Longham's home-grown opening attack of Reggie Purple and Gerald Burton, all nagging length and unswerving accuracy, formed a formidable combination. I often wondered why they didn't get lured to a higher sphere, like Beeston's tall and athletic paceman Mike Draper. He answered the predictable call from Dereham after a series of impressive village displays.

There were a few examples of useful players getting drawn into controversial transfers among our cluster of smaller clubs. I recall Beeston stalwarts passing the hat round to buy a pair of cricket boots for a Fransham product suddenly out of step with his home environment. New footwear was the "fee" for his services.

I was the youngest scorer by far on the local scene but treated respectfully by most names-and-numbers companions. My favourite was Mrs

King of Longham, who apart from ensuring I got an early choice of cakes at teatime before ravenous players moved in, listened patiently to my regular moans about Longham gamesmanship with an understanding smile. She said she would have a quiet word with them before we met again...

Perhaps I knew instinctively that the pen would always be mightier than the sward in my cause. Even so, there were raised eyebrows at grammar school over my reputation as a budding statistician. Hardly surprising in view of my abject failure to make any discernible progress in maths lessons.

I hadn't a clue about logarithms, vulgar fractions or any theory from Pythagoras. Yet I revelled in working out the latest Beeston batting and bowling averages. I was equally at home chalking up for darts matches. It had to be put down to flourishing naturally in relaxed social and

Cricket resumed at Aldborough Green near Cromer in 1947. The green was re-levelled after being ploughed up during the war.

sporting atmospheres while algebra and geometry tests in bleak classroom conditions cut off supplies of intelligence to the brain.

My Hamond's Grammar School cricket playing career at Swaffham scarcely moved beyond ordinary level although boundless enthusiasm for the roles of 12th man and scorer did bring unexpected glories. I stepped into the breach for a fixture at Paston Grammar School in North Walsham when one of our under-15 stars when down with chicken pox.

I clung to a neat catch at mid-off after a series of unlucky misfields – I found the only bumps on the ground without trying – and remained unbeaten on nought (facing three wayward deliveries) when the final wicket fell at the other end. We lost by quite a few but I escaped most of the blame.

When it became abundantly clear that my passion for cricket was highly unlikely to lead to any outstanding personal achievements on the field, I accepted a place among the many who watch and admire with only a hint of envy and then occasionally help the talented to feel even better about themselves in an increasingly competitive world.

Our grass-roots game still needs stoically cheerful characters prepared to advertise their weaknesses without letting go of genuine love and respect for something which has kept them company since childhood.

My village scorebooks days – even those etched in mild acrimony over blasted Longham's superiority – helped me find a lasting relationship with true Norfolk community values.

I picked up the art of diplomacy as a batsman returned from the middle with a highly dubious lbw decision to his name. As he swore he wasn't out, I made sympathetic noises rather than invite him to inspect my book for indisputable evidence to the contrary.

I started to appreciate the value of a good temperament, allied to a sense of humour, when the odd fixture threatened to descend into open warfare. "Bring back the Home Guard!" and "This'll look good in the paper!" usually soothed tempers... along with a quiet reminder that valuable drinking time was being wasted.

I used interesting facts and figures concerning others to camouflage complete absence of any concerning myself. I never had a batting average worth working out during my 18 formative years in the village and bowled only twice in proper matches when results had long been decided. But I talked a good game and sounded knowledgeable at the annual meeting.

I came to recognise the architectural outline of a host of rural pubs, even in poor light, and to know which ones had a piano in the bar without venturing through the door. I sent crisps sales soaring but learnt to dine alone when Beeston's brave boys upset the odds.

And I can still boast that I never fell off the back of a lorry.

SWARM GOING

What do Old Trafford in 1887 and Shropham in 1982 have in common? Press your buzzers if you know - both grounds saw play held up by swarms of bees.

At Lancashire headquarters so many bees flew on during the match against Surrey that players were forced to take refuge in the pavilion. The more recent epic between Shropham and Hales in south-west Norfolk was also bedevilled by the little creatures and play was held up five minutes either side of the tea interval.

Any honey in the sandwiches?

WICKET WIT

A young cricketer with public school experience moved to a rural area of Norfolk and was picked to play in the big local derby away to the neighbouring village.

He travelled on his own, arrived early and met a rustic leaning on the gate to the field of combat.

"Should be a close one ...what?"

"Dunt reckon so atorl ... we'll marder yer."

"Jolly well see about that, my good man! Now tell me, who scores most of your runs?"

"Billy Jenkins, the cowman's boy. Allus good fer fifty at least."

"And who, may I inquire, takes most of your wickets?"

"Why, I dew, marster."

"You, At your age? An opening bowler..... ?"

"Blarst me, no bor ....I'm th'umpire!"

WATCH THE BIRDIE!

One swallow may not make a summer – but it can cause a big flutter all the same. That's the message behind a true story from Derek Bales of Stoke Holy Cross.

He recalled a match in August, 1955, when Stoke-Dunston CC played at Fritton, near Hempnall. "During the Fritton innings, Stanley Prior – known to all as Bossie – was fielding in the covers when he caught a swallow. He always insisted it was a deliberate act and not a reflex action.

"The match stopped while all the players examined the startled bird which was released after about a minute."

Derek began playing for Dunston in 1951. His last full season came in 1980 and he was secretary for 30 years. In 1957, Stoke Holy Cross formed a separate club while Dunston continued on the old ground.

FOUR

FAMILY FLAIR

I spent too long in the deep worrying about being the odd one out in a set of brothers weaned on village cricket. It wasn't fair to be stuck in the middle like that, a sort of well-intentioned joker in the pack, a harmless aberration on an otherwise impressive scorecard.

Yes, I could talk a good game and spice it up with plenty of statistics from parish pitch to Test Match arena. I became an enthusiastic sports reporter and avid follower of the summer game at all levels. But my brothers' actions always spoke much louder than my words.

Maurice Skipper

Older siblings Maurice, still better known as Digger, and Malcolm, who answers readily to his lifelong nickname of Sprat, both had to temper early Beeston exploits with acceptance that duties on the farm, especially at harvest and milking times, could take precedence on some sunswept afternoons and evenings.

Younger brothers Colin and Mick settled into the family routine with ease. I practised with all four of them down the yard and on the orchard. Somehow, my cover drives and late cuts never matched theirs for

Malcolm Skipper - Single-Wicket Champion 1967

timing or placement. Sadly, my craftiest spinners and fastest straight ones finished up on the road or over the wall.

That didn't stop them trying to push me on to higher levels but I suspect they knew all the while that book and biro would invariably look more comfortable in my grasp than bat or ball. To their credit, they never sniggered when desperate little experiments, like bowling slow off a long run or batting with my cap covering one eye, failed to bring about any appreciable improvements.

Oldest brother Maurice's versatility became a big talking point during my early days as village scorer. He bowled left-arm but batted right-handed, a combination bound to prompt lively comment out in the middle and among spectators.

"Does he umpire with his feet?" inquired one bright spark at Gateley in a way that suggested he'd just witnessed one of the most remarkable double-acts in Norfolk sporting history.

Big brother turned in countless impressive spells of medium-pace bowling and collected useful runs as a free-hitting batsman. He recalls career-best figures of 10 for 21 against North Pickenham with a rueful smile. "They were all out for 42 – but Beeston still managed to lose."

Umpiring incidents were common enough in those days when clubs sent out one of their own to officiate. Impartiality and knowledge of the rules could be thrown open to question when important decisions were called for, although a relaxed attitude and good laugh might be enough to diffuse some delicate situations.

A mixture of disbelief and loud guffaws greeted a series of apparently debatable decisions in a match when Beeston entertained Castle Acre. "They had Des Creed umpiring and he appeared to be very generous in upholding a number of appeals as we batted" said Maurice.

"We had Wilfred Cross standing at the other end. His sons Ralph and Ray finished up in the same crease and it seemed a mere formality when Castle Acre appealed for a run-out. But Wilfred was so angry at what had happened to earlier batsman he refused to send either son on his way!"

Malcolm Skipper.

Peace and a semblance of harmony were restored eventually but that game when the umpiring "creed" finished up at "cross" purposes still provokes chuckles among those at the heart of it.

Brother Malcolm (this is beginning to sound like a monastery register) dug in as a steady, dependable batsman and handy tweaker from the age of 14 until he called it a day at 58. He played for Beeston, Lexham, Tittleshall, Gressenhall, Beetley and the Black Sheep Charity XI.

He captained Lexham, Tittleshall and Beetley – and tested those leadership qualities against me when I took BBC Radio Norfolk teams to Beetley in the 1980s and early 1990s. Honours were about even, although Malcolm compiled a typically patient 58 in one of the best knocks of his career.

He put on 80 with brother-in-law Lennie Sayer for Lexham against a strong Fakenham line-up and went on to claim two runners-up medals in the prestigious Dr Fisher Cup knockout competition.

Pairs of Beeston brothers were prolific during his early days: "Apart from Digger and me, we had George and Harry Elliott, Eddie and Mike Garner and Ray and Ralph Cross."

Colin Skipper.

He recalled how big brother took 9 for 11 for Beeston at Necton one evening in a knockout tie... and then Albert Hudson claimed 8 for 10 the next. "We drank the Tuns pub dry!"

Brother Colin, probably the most naturally gifted of the clan, made his Beeston debut as a schoolboy and went on to impress as a free-flowing batsman for Swaffham, Costessey and Marlingford. He also guested for Ingham, one of the county's leading clubs, in bank holiday fixtures, catching the eye with unbeaten 40s, and brought much-needed flair to Radio Norfolk's order in those Beetley challenges.

Biggest disappointment of those fruitful summers came with a score of 99 not out for Marlingford against Dereham Hockey Club. He thought he'd reached a ton in hitting the winning run. "But when the scores were totted up at the end, it became clear I had finished one short and so didn't get on the honours board."

Brother Mick performed enthusiastically from 1974 until 1981, mostly for Tittleshall where he regularly helped prepare the wicket and mowed the outfield. A shepherd's hut served as changing room... "and there were plenty of sheep droppings in the deep!" A later version of Cowpat Corner?

Mainly a lower-order batsman, Mick remembers with keen satisfac-

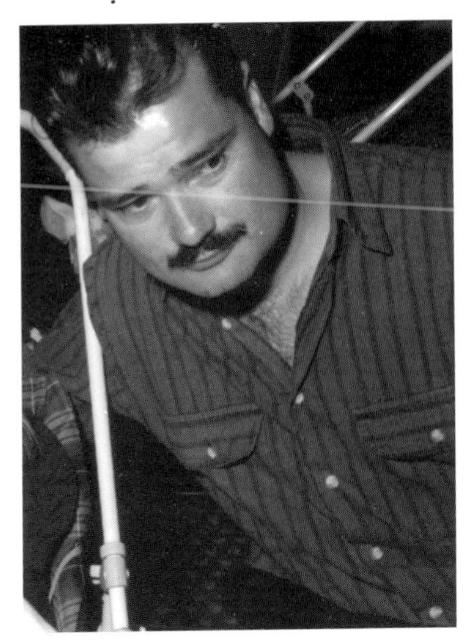

Mick Skipper.

tion a defiant 24 at North Elmham which included three cracking fours to the tennis courts. A bitter-sweet hat-trick demands an encore as well: "I was playing for FMC pea viners at Fakenham Grammar School on a summer afternoon when I took a hat-trick. But much of the joy disappeared as I suffered an injury while picking up the third victim." His knee went out of joint.

Mick also made bold marks on the martial arts scene in Tai Kwando.

Just bare outlines of how four Skipper brothers played their parts in establishing a strong family tradition on local cricket grounds. And then there were Skipper sisters getting in on the act.......

Beeston's sporting instincts came to a fresh peak in July, 1963, when the fairer sex challenged the village lads at their own game. I helped set up this intriguing contest, acted as scorer (I still knew my rightful place) and contributed a full report to the Dereham and Fakenham Times.

The lads went in first, batting with the opposite hand they used normally. One poor chap was clean bowled while he waited for the umpire to give him a guard, but the ladies begged him to stay put. They wanted no charity with a big gallery looking on.

Margaret Watson clung on to a superbly-judged catch on the village hall boundary. Wendy Skipper – she and sister Marina unfurled the fresh family banner – made a skier look simple at mid-wicket.

The men had to work overtime for a total of 93. Opposition hopes soared when wicket-keeper Dorothy Burrell, who had played for Fakenham Women, tucked away anything short to the legside. The men, as well as bowling with the "wrong" arm, had to catch with the "wrong" hand.

As dark clouds gathered menacingly overhead, the girls sportingly decided not to appeal against the light. They went down gamely by 34 runs, but a stirring village occasion was destined for a full page in the sporting scrapbook.

With more Skippers to the fore as I looked on admiringly.

Beeston Belles rang out a cricketing challenge to local lads in 1963.

CENTREFOLD

The worst cricket captain is the one who sends you out to bat in the middle of a hat-trick.

CLOCKING OFF

Chris Sugden, turning out for Keswick College, was sharing a last-wicket stand at Hindringham. "It must have been a last-wicket stand because I was batting. Not that I couldn't hit the ball. I just didn't hit it off the square very often.

"The game was being played to time so at 7 o'clock our captain went to shake hands with his opposite number to accept a draw. But the home captain shook his head. 'We always go by the church clock' he said, pointing.

"We looked and, sure enough, it read 6.45. So we were forced to bat another 15 minutes to achieve our draw. But I kicked myself afterwards.

"I'm convinced that if we'd looked in the opposite direction we'd have seen another clock, reading 7.15, for use should the home team find themselves in a similar predicament."

STRIKE BOWLER

Brothers Douglas and Bob Millar were in action for Gothic Wanderers against Smallburgh at Eaton Park in Norwich in the mid-1960s when one of them turned dramatically into a strike bowler...

Bob sent down a shortish, rising delivery which struck the batsman on the thigh. He started hopping around in some discomfort. It was only when they saw the batsmen reach into his pocket that they realised what had happened,

He had a box of matches – presumably not of the safety variety – which had spontaneously combusted and set fire to his trousers! The incident finished up on the front page of the *Daily Express* in the Just Fancy That column.

Yes, "Fiery" Bob Millar really did earn national recognition when he set the local scene alight!

JUST LIKE LIFE

The Rev Derek Bream, vicar of St Just-near-Trunch, is an acute observer of the local scene. Here's Derek's Fifth Letter to the Truncheons delivered by Chris Sugden and Sid Kipper from their literary collection, Cod Pieces:

Life's like that, isn't it? Only the other day I was driving through Dunston when I saw a cricket match being played. I do so love to watch the flannelled fools, so I immediately got out of my little VW Beetle, Betsy, to watch.

Of course, if I had the chance to do it all over again, I would stop the car first. But not to worry. As it turned out, that barn was just as effective in stopping Betsy as her brakes. If not more so. And after the cricketers had pulled Betsy out of the barn and re-housed the pigs they carried on with their jolly game.

And then it struck me. No, not a lusty six hit out of the middle of the bat straight back over the bowler's head. Although it might as well have been that because I was too deep in revelation to have noticed such a petty distraction.

What I realised there is that life is like a game of cricket, isn't it? Sometimes it's all bats, and sometimes it's all balls, but we each have our place in the field of life, and we're all hoping to score. But when the great umpire in the sky raises his finger, we'll know that our innings is at an end. And, when the game has been played out, what will it say about us in the scorebook of life?

Will it be full of fours and sixes and quickly scampered singles? Or will it simply say "stumped, nought."?

You see what I'm saying, don't you? Well, if you do, I wish you'd write and tell me. Because I fear I've rather lost my thread. But in the meantime, just remember this. If God had meant me to see what I was saying, He'd have put me on the telly, not the radio.

FIVE

CAISTER COMRADES

My earliest days as a fearless newspaper reporter in Thetford and Dereham afforded no clear chance to pick up the threads of a flimsy playing career. A short spell in the town embracing overspill from London coincided with the coldest winter since 1740, while a free transfer to the heart of Norfolk brought regular weekend duties with notebook and typewriter.

I did manage to feed a growing appetite for covering sports fixtures, however, and volunteered eagerly to place football, darts and cricket on top of my list of specialist subjects. Dereham and district provided a lively grounding for a budding scribe keen to avoid too many dog shows, garden fetes and floral exhibitions.

My move to Yarmouth in the mid 1960s found a cheerful refuge for revived ambitions on the performing front as Caister Cricket Club welcomed an occasional spinner – one delivery might turn every three overs on a good day and a helpful pitch – with few batting or fielding pretensions. They tolerated my shortcomings for over 20 seasons.

Yarmouth Mercury colleague David Wakefield, a gritty and accurate medium-pace bowler (and keen supporter of Peterborough in the soccer season), started the tradition of local reporters turning out for Caister after attending their annual dinner and sampling an appealing brand of comradeship and fun. "They don't take it too seriously" he confided in a manner that suggested even someone as average as me might squeeze into the team.

I received an immediate call to action from jovial captain Eddie Brown after just one audition in the nets. He did admit some years later that a reputation as a daring (bad) card player and useful (shameless) pub entertainer had as much to do with early selection as any modest (well-hidden) talents straining to be noticed.

My social skills could come in handy on regular retreats to the pub for a light-hearted inquest into another unlucky defeat and I could be relied on to make the best of a bad job with carefully-crafted match reports in the paper. Caister's ability to go down with a smile, even to the point of staging an old-time music hall in the bar to salute the winners, turned many a one-sided afternoon into a memorable evening.

I threatened to peak too early out in the middle with three victims in four deliveries in a golden summer session in front of Somerleyton Hall, the ideal setting for someone clearly on the way to class status. A career-best 22 not out (three slices over slips, a blind hoick over square-leg, a thick edge past the wicket-keeper and two overthrows for a tame push to mid-on) heralded all-round credentials in the making soon after at Filby.

The latter occasion against close rivals was also notable for the disappearance of my new white pullover during inevitable celebrations in the village pub. It resurfaced the following summer in the same establishment, much the worse for wear after being used to dry glasses.

The mystery of my disappearing trousers a couple of summers later on one of our more raucous trips to Weston in Hertfordshire was solved the same evening. But not before I had sought sanctuary in bushes behind the pub as local Women's Institute members arrived back by bus from their annual outing. They parted company without too much cheek from Norfolk tourists.

Caister Revellers - David Wakefield, Keith Skipper and Mike Farman toast a Caister victory

The Weston safaris assumed legendary status for mixing sporting business with cultural pleasures. Fellow Yarmouth newshound Mike Farman, a big chap with a big voice, raised the tone with his moving impression of Constance Shackcloth singing Rule Britannia.

Hardly a dry glass in the house. Inhibitions were sent scurrying while players, umpires, tea ladies, spectators, pub regulars and slightly perplexed visitors attracted by the glorious noise unfurled the patriotic flag and allowed themselves to be coaxed into the world of song.

Mr Wakefield, mainly responsible for such rich press representation at this irreverent version of Last Night of the Proms, kept it going with his renowned versatility at the piano. I knew when to strike with an emotional rendition of the Norfolk anthem, Hev Yew Gotta Loight, Boy? Perfect excuse for impromptu elocution lessons in a convivial climate.

Most outstanding playing feat of my Caister years was tarnished slightly by one of the more crushing setbacks in the club's history. With several of our best players unavailable, I answered an emergency call to arms against Swardeston, fast emerging as a major power, in a Norfolk Junior Cup-tie.

We travelled in a mood of cheerful resignation. They piled up getting on for 400 runs. Captain Peter Thomas plundered about half of them, towering sixes constantly threatening to put the ice-cream van out of action on the edge of his village green. We urged him to cool down – but the heat remained on our wilting attack.

Remarkably, in the midst of all this carnage I claimed six wickets for 72 with my apologetic turners – including a hat-trick! Swardeston, who shot us out for 85 in reply, presented me with a smart club tie when I accepted an invitation to speak at their end-of-term celebrations and insisted they had not gifted me those three successive victims as some sort of consolation prize.

I enjoyed a long and fruitful relationship with Swardeston while based in Norwich as a sports reporter for both the *Eastern Evening News* and *Eastern Daily Press* in the 1970s. I followed local cricket clubs making sorties into fresh areas of combat. Norwich outfits Wanderers and Barleycorns made telling marks on national knockout competitions, but battlers from Bradfield and Swardeston collected even bigger plaudits for their progress in the Haig National Village stakes.

I relished the biggest rural uprising for many a summer as Swardeston hit the road to reach nerve-tingling later stages of the Haig competition. It all sprang to life at Audley End in Essex on a sunswept Sunday afternoon. The lovely country house provided a perfect backcloth for the village faithful strung out along the riverbank like Red Indians who'd found a new reservation.

For several weekends after that, Swardeston turned into a ghost parish as cricketers played Pied Piper to an old-fashioned community spirit we feared had been bowled out. It reminded me of outings to Dereham on

August Bank Holiday Monday in the 1950s for the Mid-Norfolk Shield Final, ranking alongside our annual trip to the seaside as a summer ritual for village sharing.

Mike Farman rubbing shoulders with former England stars Denis Compton and Ted Dexter at a charity match between Fleet Street newspapers. Partly hidden in the background is Scout, racing correspondent of the Daily Express. *Mike recalls "Dexter hit me for three successive fours in the first over but I got him caught in the slips in the third."*

With more than a passing nod towards those good old days, I used my privileged position on the local press to organise and publicise an annual Evergreens fixture for those determined to defy the passing seasons. Farmer Eddie Symonds set a useful example, keeping wicket for Rackheath into his 80th year!

Back to the Caister beat and a couple of other personal milestones worth savouring. I collected the only medal of my playing days in 1983 as a member of the victorious Neave Plate line-up. And I returned to dear old Dereham to play on that sacred town turf in a Norfolk Junior Cup semi-final. Caister lost - but I had a bowl and lingered at the bar long enough to suggest I was worthy of the setting.

Most Caister outings during my time with the club were tied up more with pints and party pieces than with points and progress. Even so, there were clear signs of a new competitive edge being sharpened by the formation and rapid expansion of leagues and the introduction of new cup contests.

Some of us mourned the demise of the good old friendly, mainly because the average performer could be given a run in those fixtures when results weren't all-important. I collected far more friends and yarns than wickets and runs... and I suspect several amiable colleagues and familiar opponents were happy to do the same

One of the most shattering incidents during those cheerful Caister years was recalled on a visit to Garboldisham for a mardle with members of the local history group and their friends. I played several times in this south Norfolk village and fully expected a deputation from the past with warmest thanks for not causing them any trouble.

It duly arrived – with a reminder of what a rugged Garboldisham batsman achieved in a return fixture at Caister. A towering six smashed through the window of a house beyond the playing field. As a budding diplomat and dispensable bowler, I was volunteered to pop round, apologise and retrieve the ball.

It had entered perilously close to a child eating tea in a high chair, bounced off the table and finished up in a fruit bowl on the sideboard. The lady of the house wore a glazed look as she counted her oranges and asked what I wanted.

"Please, can we have our ball back?" seemed an utterly inadequate response. The child in the high chair chuckled and called for afters.

I emphasised that a visiting player who didn't know his own strength was responsible for this sudden teatime interruption but the home club would gladly pay for all damage. She didn't request counselling, threaten to sue or call in the United Nations. I returned to the fray with fruit of my labours.

My elevation to the post of Sunday captain, albeit during a period when suitable candidates were thin on the ground, allowed me to pursue an "everybody gets a turn" policy, both to encourage youngsters and to thank those old-fashioned virtues of comradeship and fun for allowing me to defy an obvious shortage of talent.

I travelled to many matches with old friend Fred Leak, a sound batsman, smart wicket-keeper and earnest student of the game. He threatened to make me walk home several times following lbw decisions against him when I answered the call to shoulder umpiring duties for a while. He never did carry out that threat – but repeated it whenever we happened to be batting together for the Caister cause.

Fred operated under the delusion that I could run as fast as him. His excitable call of "three!" had been voted most optimistic war cry in the club's history well before my stuttering efforts reduced it simply to a number for ordering pints of shandy for yourself and two admirers.

Dashing Fred, and one or two others who were sharpish out of the blocks, eventually accepted the proud boast by old lifeboatmnen that" Caister men never turn back!" need not apply to every landlubber turning out for the local cricket team.

Lack of studs in my boots and too much smoking could leave energetic partners stranded as I reversed breathlessly to the safety of my crease. It has been claimed I nearly got lapped twice while waiting for a drive to reach the boundary against Brisley.

I willed it over the line and told the chap panting at the other end to show more faith in my timing.

GOOD CALL

Did you hear about the Norfolk cricketer whose answerphone insisted he was not out?

THE SECOND INNINGS

As I walked out another day, through meadow and through thicket,
I saw a maid I'd met before, who loved the game of cricket.
Said she "Since you are in the field, you are the very fellow;
I'll set myself against you now, if you will "wield the willow."

Since she was such a sporting lass I surely couldn't reject her;
And so I now prepared to play, by donning a protector.
Her bouncers very soon I faced, as past my ears they whipped;
She made them swing, the tension rose, and she removed her slip.

Now she went to it with a will, all well up to the bat;
I middled it most sweetly, and she had to smile at that.
Oh I was really scoring now, the nudges, pulls and pats,
But then I strayed out of the crease, and thus came my collapse.

She had me stumped, and I was out, her turn had come to face;
She set herself with feet apart, and cried "Let's see some pace;
Let's see a good length, sir" she cried, "All in the channel, straight,
And I'd appreciate it, sir, if you would swing it late."

I teased her with my slower ball, and she stepped out to meet it;
The way she wound up for the shot showed how she meant to treat it.
But as it reached her, so it turned, her eyes were full of doubt;
I surprised her with my follow-through, and so I caught her out.

Well who had won? We had to ask the Vicar to decide.
And when we told him what had passed he said we'd best be tied.
Well often now we go to play, and never mind the winning;
For always we look forward to the outings and the innings.

From the singing of Sid Kipper

SIX

TOP OF THE BILL

It was the biggest tingle of my Coronation Year sporting spectacular – a Norfolk battler at the crease as England won back the Ashes from the Aussies for the first time in two decades. Yes, Denis Compton cracked the clinching runs at the Oval, but the chap at the other end from our most famous home-grown cricketing clan took pride of place in my 1953 scrapbook.

Bill Edrich, arguably the finest sportsman the county has produced, was a brilliant back-foot batsman, a superb hooker and player of offspin. His courage was legendary; Alan Hill, his first-class biographer, provides the perfect close-of-play summary: "His spectacular life mingled the constant kindness and care of a true countryman with the bravado of a born crusader. The heroism, which gained him the DFC in the Second World War, brought him enduring respect as a formidable adversary at cricket. He was a patriot first and foremost.

"Playing for England and fighting for England without blemish or shame were his priorities."

Bill Edrich on parade for England

Bill was born in 1916 at Lingwood, eight miles east of Norwich, into an old-established family of farmers already known for their cricketing prowess. Three of Bill's

Edrich family on parade in 1947

brothers also played the first-class game, Eric and Geoffrey for Lancashire and Brian for Kent and Glamorgan. Cousin John made his big mark for Surrey and England. Over the years teams made up entirely of the Edrich family played a host of popular fixtures.

As a 16-year-old pupil at Bracondale School in Norwich in 1932, Bill marched out to face the All-India tourists at Lakenham with Norfolk floundering on 21 for 5. He made 20 in 40 minutes. For the first time, Edrich defiance was written into the records.

Although 2,000 runs in each of three pre-war seasons marked his outstanding talents, there were lingering doubts about his Test match temperament. A nightmare baptism against the Australians in 1938 – just 67 runs in six innings – continued in South Africa the following year with just 21 runs in five innings. But England skipper Wally Hammond kept faith in the young man from Norfolk. In the "timeless" fifth Test Edrich piled up a morale-lifting 240.

That unquenchable spirit on the field was soon put to the test in the wartime arena. Bill, as a Pilot Officer in the celebrated 107 Squadron based at Great Massingham, took his Blenheim on several horrendously dangerous operations over Germany, including the first daylight raid on the Ruhr.

"Billy boy, we'd follow you anywhere" exclaimed one Canadian flyer. Edrich won the Distinguished Flying Cross and led other hazardous attacks on heavily-fortified German installations. These death-defying operations were to have a profound effect on his future life, every day emerging as a bonus to be relished.

One raid was mounted only hours before Bill's squadron were due to play a cricket match against a Massingham XI. Edrich flew through a storm of fire and made it back safely. Two crews did not. Their places were filled by substitutes and the game went ahead even though the memory of so much death and destruction was never far away.

Poignantly recalling that cricket encounter, Edrich wrote: "Every now and then would come the old accustomed cry... OWZATT!... and then one's mind would flicker off to the briefing and to joking with a pal whose broken body was now washing in the long, cold tides, and one saw again his machine cartwheeling down, flaming from nose to tail, and then a ball would roll fast along the green English turf, and in the distance the village clock would strike and the mellow echoes would ring through the lazy air of that perfect summer afternoon."

After the war Bill's devil-may-care lifestyle enlivened the austerity gloom, above all in partnership with his Middlesex "twin" Denis Compton during that rhapsodic, record-breaking summer of 1947 when Bill scored 3,539 runs and Compton 3,816. How fitting they should be together six seasons later when the sun of Ashes success shone over the Oval.

Bill's high spirits did upset some in authority, however, and he was dropped from the 1951 tour of Australia. Restored to favour, he played a major part in Coronation Year.

During 1952 in fading light at Lord's he was felled by a bouncer from Frank "Typhoon" Tyson, reckoned by no less an authority than Sir

Donald Bradman to be the fastest bowler he had ever seen. Edrich's cheekbone was fractured, but to the astonishment of all he returned to the crease next morning, his jaw in a sling, his eyes all but closed by massive facial bruising.

Tyson's "welcome back" was another bouncer. "Believe it or not, Bill tried to hook it" recalled Frank. "You simply could not intimidate him."

After retirement from first-class cricket in 1958, he returned to his native county and led Norfolk for 11 seasons. "Seldom can the enjoyment of the players have been better communicated to spectators, seldom can a side have had a better team spirit" said former Norfolk secretary David Armstrong.

When he played for Norfolk between 1932 and 1936, Edrich scored 2,160 runs and took 119 wickets. By the end of his second spell with the county, those figures stood at 8,308 and 417 respectively.

Bill was also a talented soccer player. He had made his Football league debut for Spurs against Blackpool in 1935 but was forced out of the game six years later by strained knee ligaments.

He married no less than five times – "Bill was always falling in love" said his old friend Trevor Bailey. Former Middlesex colleague John Warr, asked to attend one of Bill's weddings, recalled being told he needed an invitation to get in. "Invitation?" he queried. "I've got a season ticket for Bill's weddings!"

Alan Hill said his character juxtaposed honourable and wanton elements. Caring, kind and never deliberately hurtful, he noted, beyond the heartbreaks of the estrangements was the remarkable legacy of lingering affection. "The tender forgiveness of Bill's ladies in retirement is a testimony to an infuriating but disarming man."

Action at Ingham. Bill Edrich attacks the bowling of John Tythcott. Billy Rose is the batsman at the other end.

National journalist Ian Wooldridge wrote: "Bill Edrich epitomised the peculiarly British breed of incurable scallywag. He loved life too much to harbour grudges, sustain feuds or niggle opponents, with whom, like as not, he'd been out on the tiles at the close of play. But there was a bottom line to the roistering. You had to be there before start of play next day. Then, hungover or otherwise, you had to fight."

Five years after his death in 1986, a stand at his beloved Lord's was named after him and dedicated to his memory – next to one similarly dedicated to Denis Compton. Sentinels of a remembrance of a glorious era when a Norfolk farmer's boy went to cricket headquarters to reap such a rich harvest.

Bill Edrich fought for England on the hallowed turf and in the war-torn skies. He led my parade of Coronation Year sporting heroes... and came home to Norfolk for a glorious Indian summer. He ruled with evangelical fervour and infused young disciples with a do-or-die spirit to inspire a big upturn in the county's fortunes.

One of Bill's last appearances for Norfolk came in the Gillette Cup first-round tie against Middlesex at Lord's in April, 1970. He made top score of 36 out of a total of 117. Middlesex were easy winners by 147 runs – but it was an occasion of overflowing sentiment as the old warrior returned.

"For one glorious hour he disdainfully rolled back the years and showed why he is part of the legend of Lord's" wrote Alex Bannister. My old colleague Bryan Stevens, also there to file a report for the *Eastern Daily Press* on a player he had watched and admired for so many summers ... "Edrich, applauded all the way to the wicket, took some time to get off the mark. Gradually he moved into gear and brought the memories flooding back."

The last six balls of Bill's innings yielded 22 runs, including two sixes. His reign in Norfolk ended in 1971, 39 years after walking out as a resolute schoolboy at Lakenham.

His death following a St George's Day celebration came a month after his 70th birthday. Sadness in cricket circles was compounded by the passing of another great player, Jim Laker, only 24 hours earlier. Rivalry between the two and their fiercely competitive duels is enshrined in the folklore of the game.

Celebrations which had marked Edrich's 70th birthday prompted Ian Wooldridge to suggest any definitive profile of Bill would be better suited to The Lancet than Wisden.

"He played and fought with old-fashioned virtues; that you were never beaten until they'd battered the last breath out of your body.

"He was convinced that to be born English was to have drawn a winning ticket in life."

And that ticket became even more precious when it was stamped in Norfolk.

A ROLL MODEL

Ray Fenn rolled back the years to recall a cautionary tale from the late 1940s.

"Shotesham cricket pitch was in the middle of the 'hoss midder' behind the farm close to where I still live. My father was employed there and one spring day was engaged in rolling an adjacent field in preparation for drilling.

"He was accosted by the rather haughty Hon Sec of the local cricket club ... 'Ay say, my man, run your roller over the cricket square when you have a moment.' Father declined, saying he had two reasons for not doing as asked. Actually, I suspect three if you count not being called anybody's 'good man'.

"He said that in the first place he was employed by the farmer and not the cricket club.

Before he could raise his second objection Hon Sec stormed off... returning in triumph with a note from the farmer stating it was in order for him to do it if he had time.

"Having finished the field, he smoked a contemplative Woodbine while deciding how best to tackle the job. He felt it best to work diagonally across the square and in two or three passes the job was done. You may recall he had told Hon Sec, who didn't stop to listen, that he had two objections to rolling the pitch...

"The second objection was that he had reservations about the suitability of a rib-roll, pulled by a tractor on spud wheels, to produce a surface even for village cricket!"

VILLAGE CRICKET

Flowing together by devious channels
From farm and brickyard, forest and dene,
Thirteen men in glittering flannels
Move to their stations out on the green.
Long-limbed wagoner, stern, unbudging,
Stands like a rock behind the bails.
Dairyman umpire, gravely judging,
Spares no thought for his milking pails.
Bricklayer bowls a perfect length,
Grocer snicks and sneaks a run
Law, swiping with all his strength,
Is caught by chemist at mid-on.
Two to the boundary, a four and a six,
Put the spectators in fear of their lives;
Shepherd the slogger is up to his tricks,
Blithely unwary of weans and wives.
Lord of the manor makes thirty-four,
Parson contributes, smooth and trim,
A cautious twelve to the mounting score;
Leg-before wicket disposes of him.
Patient, dramatic, serious, genial,
From over to over the game goes on
Weaving a pattern of hardy perennial
Civilisation under the sun.

Gerald Bullet

SEVEN

FULLER TALENT

While cricket and football formed the twin towers of my boyhood sporting stadium, I did get excited about boxer Jem Mace... when I discovered he was born in my home village and went on to become world heavyweight champion.

Mace (1831-1910) has a white stone memorial in Beeston churchyard. It was retrieved from a Norwich stonemason's yard and moved to his home patch by "A few of his old friends" in 1976. He took boxing from its rough roots as an outlaw sport to the global stage.

He claimed the world crown in New Orleans and at the height of his fame included Wyatt Earp and Charles Dickens among celebrity acquaintances. He was a Victorian superstar.

Only natural, then, that I should drop the Mace name into any conversation when trying to build up Beeston's chances in sporting combat, especially if opponents hailed from the neighbouring parishes of Longham and Litcham. It didn't prevent a series of painful knock-out blows – but we took satisfaction in Mace's ability to soak up punishment before coming out on top.

It was no less intriguing to find out a bit later that another giant of the Victorian sporting world hailed from another small Norfolk community. And he was good enough a cricketer to be mentioned in the same hallowed breath as Dr W G Grace.

Fuller Pilch was born in Horningtoft, five miles south-east of Fakenham, in 1804, third son of Nathaniel Pilch and Frances Fuller, who were married in Brisley, not far away, and later returned to live there.

Fuller followed in the confident footsteps of his two elder brothers, Nathaniel and William, to become a professional cricketer, the most famous batsman of his era. His first appearance at Lord's came in a three-day match in July, 1820, playing for Norfolk as a teenager rich in promise.

Fuller Pilch, giant of the Victorian sporting world.

At over six foot, he was very tall for his age – mother's tasty Norfolk dumplings did the trick – and his batting was stylish and characterised by his forward play. His long forward plunge could crush the best bowling before it had a chance to shoot, or rise or do mischief by forcing a catch. It became famous as "The Pilch Poke".

Pilch was in great demand by 1827. He played in England games against Sussex, his first match for Players versus Gentlemen, for Leicester against Sheffield (twice) and again at Sheffield for England. He also turned out at Lord's for Right-handed v Left-handed and for England v the B's (Bowyer, Bray, Beagley etc).

He returned to Norwich around 1829 to manage the Norwich ground and a local pub on Bracondale Hill. At this time he played for Norfolk against the MCC.

It was always going to be difficult for Norfolk to hang on to such an outstanding performer and Pilch was lured to Kent in 1836 by an offer of £100 a year. He went on to play top-level cricket until he was 51 and played a major part in restoring Kent as a real force in the game.

Incidentally, when Pilch went to Kent he took with another useful Norfolk cricketer in William Stearman of Aldborough, near Cromer. His batting won him a place in the Kent line-up for four seasons.

While on parade with Norfolk, Fuller Pilch scored handsome victories over Yorkshireman Tom Marsden, the single-wicket champion. Pilch won by an innings and 70 runs in Norwich and by 127 runs in Sheffield. Before Pilch went to Kent, Norfolk beat Yorkshire in what was probably the first county match to be played in Norwich. Pilch made 87 not out and 73. Next year he shone once more against the Tykes, piling up an unbeaten 157 in Norfolk's second innings.

In retirement Pilch kept the Saracen's Head in Canterbury. He's reputed to have refused all appeals for credit as he did for lbw when umpiring. "Bowl 'em out!" he would scornfully cry. One of the colourful legends to follow him is that he carried a scythe around with his cricket gear, doing an impression of Old Father Time to mow the outfield before the match began.

He was a star long before W G Grace. The Earl of Bessborough, who played with the lad from Norfolk, said: "I always put Pilch and Grace in a class by themselves, and I put them very much on a level."

He died on May 1st, 1870, in Canterbury. He never married. His name strides on purposefully through sports shop connections in Norwich while David Pilch captained Norfolk in the 1970s and in all made over 200 appearances as an all-rounder for the county his illustrious ancestor served so well before switching to Kent.

Fuller Pilch also enjoys a brief innings in the novel *Flashman's Lady* by George MacDonald Fraser. Pilch is caught and bowled by Flashman in a fictional game set at Lord's between Rugby Old Boys and Kent in 1842.

I suppose the nearest I got to the Victorian era was in the very first article I wrote for the sports pages of the *Eastern Daily Press*. I went to see Arthur Cason at the end of the 1963 cricket season. He was 85 and last of the underarm bowlers of Norfolk.

He played for Mileham, starting as a lad of 16 in the mid-1890s. Mileham were top dogs in those days, winning the Mid-Norfolk Shield four years running just before the end of the century.

"I remember the old village parson doing his bit to keep us boys keen by coming up to the practice ground and offering sixpence to anyone who could knock a single wicket back." A few more puffs on his pipe and Arthur had left his Dereham home for the bank holiday atmosphere of Lexham Park in the early years of the 20th century.

"We always went there for our annual August Monday match and had a right good time with slap-up meals and all the trimmings. When old Major Keppel died his son moved to Norwich but, do you know, he still came down to play with us, arriving in his horse and buggy. Real gentleman he was."

All social barriers were flattened for a time on the cricket field. Arthur the yardman bowled to the Major's son. But there were still some players who thought they were entitled to certain privileges not mentioned in the rule-book.

David Pilch who captained Norfolk in the 1970s and made over 200 appearances as an all-rounder.

"We were playing at Weasenham Park one afternoon when they had a county wicket-keeper behind the stumps. He was really good but thought he could take the ball in front of the wicket. Nothing was said until I went into bat. I had a quiet word with him, explaining that he just couldn't do that. He turned right nasty so I complained to the umpire, schoolmaster Wigg."

Evidently, the wicket-keeper's grand reputation outweighed schoolmaster Wigg's ideas of fair play. Only comment he made was a nervous "Be quiet, Arthur, be quiet!" to the injured party. But if anything just wasn't cricket on the field of play, Arthur Cason was not afraid to point it out.

Well, it was negligence on the part of an umpire that robbed him of two victims that would have taken one Saturday afternoon tally to nine. He was bowling on Hempton Green in a strong wind when the ball appeared to him to go straight through the stumps twice without disturbing the bails.

No-one believed Arthur. So he took the ball and proved it. He had to be satisfied with what was then a career-best of 7 for 19.

"I used to put in an extra hour every night on the farm during the cricket season. It was nothing for me to walk to Wendling and back for a game of cricket."

FAIR WARNING

Norfolk village cricketer: "Howzat!"

Norfolk village umpire: "I wunt a'lookin' But if he dew it agin, he's owt!"

EIGHT

DUCKING OUT

As one who made a habit of not troubling the scorers on arrival at the batting crease, I moved with some trepidation on a journey of discovery destined to end in a memorable blank.

In my role as fearless chronicler of the local sporting scene, I knew that in 1815 a cricket team from Fakenham, Hempton and Walsingham crashed all out for nothing against the combined forces of Brisley, Dunham and Litcham. This may help explain why it wasn't until 1883 that Fakenham took the solo plunge and formed the town club.

What about more recent times? Had any sides been skittled out for nought during my years on the village circuit? Would victims be prepared to come out of the pavilion again and blink into a fresh spotlight? Was it fair to intrude into such collective grief?

Well, under-achievers showed commendable bravery and allowed me to take a steady run-up towards top of the batting flops. Upton owned up to being shot out for just four by neighbours Acle in 1952. Dudley Sutton demanded "star status" after going in at Number 10 "I was one of four to score a run – but at least I wasn't out" declared dashing Dudley.

Single-minded colleagues were Arthur Jermy, Ernie Linton and Phil Watson. Acle had knocked up 63. Then bowlers Brian Cator (6 for 3) and Peter Bayles (4 for 1) wreaked havoc.

Another local derby was recalled by John Hurren. Mattishall Juniors took on their East Tuddenham counterparts in 1947 – and dismissed them for four. This total was made up of two scoring singles and two extras in the shape of byes.

Ronnie Hewitt grabbed seven victims for a single run, including two separate hat-tricks, while Brian Proven claimed the other three for just one run.Mattishall's openers needed two deliveries to complete the rout.

Peter Emms, secretary and treasurer of the Norfolk League in its early seasons, set a new low standard with his report of Hempnall being humbled in their derby fixture against Saxlingham in the 1930s. Hempnall mustered two runs between them, Peter's grandfather, Ernest Emms, claiming 5 for 2 and Ben Thurtle 5 for 0.

Hang on, there's time for a few more devastating overs before we crown the "kings of collapse" from the early 1950s.

John Moore, former captain of Beccles Town Cricket Club, produced statistics more akin to a one-sided football match in the Waveney Valley. Beccles Caxton's second team went to nearby Gillingham and managed a miserly 13. Their despondent mood changed dramatically as railway worker Joe Lankaster and metalwork teacher Sid Sayer wreaked havoc.

Joe collected six scalps and Sid the other four while the Gillingham procession headed for the record books. They were all out for a duck, clearly a disaster worthy of national headlines. It is believed the Beccles Caxton first team wicket-keeper rang the News of the World with details of this sporting spectacular and collected £5 for his trouble.

Evidently, this was used to supply the first team with drinks for the next fortnight.

News also reached me of more lovely weather for ducks in the 1950s as Bungay bowled out Gorleston before they could get off the mark, although I still await full details.

Many minor teams across the country have been sent packing without scoring, including the line-up representing Martin Walter Ltd, a firm of vehicle builders in Folkestone, Kent. They were skittled out for nothing in May 1964.

Jean de Vere, at various times scorer, secretary and umpire to the hapless outfit, immediately volunteered to take over as coach if her husband would babysit while she supervised net practice.

One of the most celebrated individual cricket ducks in history came in July, 1960, when film star Trevor Howard rose at 5 am and travelled 180 miles to play at Buxton in Derbyshire. He was out first ball.

Now that's what I call a Brief Encounter.

Back to the Waveney Valley and how blank looks gave way to "spot the personality" as one of the fast-rising stars of television nipped home to try his luck at the crease in the 1960s.

David Paradine Frost was changing the face of media entertainment as driving force behind That Was The Week That Was, a late-night show where topical satire and irreverent attitudes towards authority became the popular norm.

His father was Methodist minister at Beccles. The boy David, a graduate of Cambridge University, took every chance to flee the studios and find sanctuary on the cricket field. David Gregson was Beccles captain at the time. "For our away games, he travelled on the back of my Vespa with cricket gear across our laps.

"It was fascinating to hear all about the build-up to the launch of TW3 on BBC Television. David turned out for us whenever he came home to Beccles. On a few occasions I had him and Jim Prior, then Minister of Agriculture, in the same side."

Clearly it did no harm to feature on the Beccles team sheet – as Sir David and Lord Jim will no doubt attest!

David Frost and captain David Gregson prepare for action with Beccles

I recall writing my own Frost report for the Dereham and Fakenham Times when he appeared in a charity match in the locality during the mid-1960s. He must have been undone by a crafty spinner to inspire my shameless headline: "That Was The Tweak That Was."

Frost also featured on a long list of stars from the worlds of first-class cricket and showbusiness to relish run-soaked matches at picturesque Ingham between the Edrich family and the Lord's Taverners. Mr Pastry and Ernie Wise rubbed shoulders with Peter Parfitt and Fred Titmus. Clement Freud and Leslie Crowther put their skills alongside those of former West Indies stalwarts Everton Weekes and Garfield Sobers.

Purists may have blanched at this unlikely mixture but crowds of up to 8,000 lapped up the carnival cricket. Anglia Television broadcast the 1964 encounter which saw Bill and Brian Edrich hit centuries in the family total of 410-7 declared. Then former England captain Peter May and Basil D'Oliveira launched a furious onslaught to lead the Taverners to victory.

Both hit centuries to make it a total of 823 runs in just four and a half hours. In 1965, when John Edrich scored 143, the day's runs added up to 809. The Taverners topped 400 – but finished one run behind!

While the Edrich clan clearly top the bill for family formations in Norfolk, exclusively fraternal ranks from the 1840s would seem to be unique. A team boasting 11 Colman brothers played special matches on local grounds, inevitably capturing many column inches in the *Norfolk News*.

Their usual batting order read: Thomas, William, Samuel, Barnard, Jeremiah, Henry, Edward, James, John, Robert and Joseph.

An extract from a report of a fixture against the Norwich Club in July, 1846 – well contested but unfinished – pointed to "the company more numerous than usual, which probably arose from the novelty of 11 brothers forming one side."

A few days later, when the lads were in action at Letheringsett Hall against 11 Gentlemen of Letheringsett and Holt, the opposition included a chap called Skipper. He dismissed two Colmans in the first innings and three in the second. However, he managed but a single on opening the reply before Jeremiah had him caught out by Samuel. Sort of perishing in the name of the Old Testament!

I recall the Battelley brothers, Barry, Ian, Martin and Chris, excelling at cricket, football, darts, table tennis and golf during my years as a reporter in and around Dereham in the early 1960s. The Wilkinsons - Wilfred, Malcolm, Marcus, Mervyn and Paul –starred in the recent history of Horsford Cricket Club. A big batch of Bidewells on the local scene as well.

Richard Shepheard reckons the Colmans would have met their match in an inter-counties clash with the Suffolk family of Tollemache, who have held their estate at Helmingham since before the Norman Conquest.

John Tollemache, 1st Baron Helmingham (1805-1890) had 24 sons and one daughter from two marriages. His lads, therefore, could field two full teams including 12th men.

"Quite what the sporting standards were I can't say but the facts are alluded to in one of two works about them. I seem to recall that cricketing adventures held some trepidation for Lionel Tollemache, who was extremely short-sighted" said Richard.

"But I gather he excelled at croquet, writing a treatise on the game. He's best remembered, however, as the Boswell of William Gladstone."

A BAT – AND A PAT

A fast-emerging talent on the Norfolk scene shared top billing in a 1951 match report from Mike Staines of Swaffham.

Mike claimed nine cheap victims in a one-sided clash at King's Lynn, but a century-making colleague destined for the big time collected most of the plaudits.

King Edward VII under-13s declared at 220 for 7 against King's Lynn Boy Scouts, with Peter Parfitt cracking 108. He later transferred to Fakenham Grammar School and went to play with distinction for Middlesex and England.

Master Staines wrecked the Scouts' batting with 9 for 8. "Peter was given a new bat for his century by headmaster Mr Sleigh. My nine wickets were worth nothing more than a pat on the back. Perhaps if I'd got all 10 I might have got more!" smiled Mike.

LAST-DITCH STAND

Pat Newman, popular landlord of Langham Bluebell pub, enjoyed a good yarn, especially when cricket was on tap.

Looking through old scorecards, he found details of a match at Cley in 1961. Langham were dismissed for 55, Pat being the only batsman to break double figures. "I was at the crease with David Saunderson, the vicar's son, and he hit the ball into a tree 'fielding' at mid-on. While the Cley players climbed the tree to retrieve the ball, we ran five!"

Cley were shot out for 27 with Mike Fuller claiming 8 for 10. He went on to make bold marks as player and groundsman for Carrow Cricket Club at Lakenham, former county headquarters.

Another memorable incident recalled by Pat from a different match at Cley. "We appealed for a run-out but the umpire from Cley standing at square-leg was missing.

"He eventually returned red-faced after emerging from a ditch on the boundary where he had been relieving himself!"

BEYOND THE PAIL

David Woodward, who played for Gillingham, near Beccles, in the late 1940s, recalled how Haddiscoe had their own format designed to help the dairy industry.

Haddiscoe always batted first by arrangement with opponents. Two cowmen worked for the farmer who owned the field where home matches were staged – and they opened the innings before moving off to milk the cows and returning, hopefully, in time for the visitors' reply.

I remember a police car hastening to Caister Cricket Club's ground on a sunny afternoon in the 1970s. We wondered who was wanted for questioning. A young member of the North Walsham team was whisked away... to answer an emergency on the farm where he worked.

ABORIGINES TOUR

The first Australian cricketers to tour England, a team of Aborigines from Victoria, met the Carrow Club in Norwich in 1868. The visitors won by an innings and 52 runs. It was to be a decade before white cricketers toured England and another 14 years before the Ashes were first contested.

SHOWING RESPECT

The village bowler was well into his run-up when a row of funeral cars passed the ground.

He stopped in his tracks, took off his cap, held it over his heart and bowed his head. The umpire was most impressed.

"You're a man who shows proper respect for the deceased" he said.

"Thass the least I could dew," replied the bowler. "Arter all, she wuz a good wife ter me fer thatty year."

NINE

MOORE OPENINGS

Derek Moore, now living in Wales, was Director of the Suffolk Wildlife Trust for 15 years. He left the Waveney Valley in 1977 after many productive seasons at the crease with Beccles and Lowestoft. Here he reflects on his "golden era" before leagues, club professionals from abroad and teams warming up in tracksuits and baseball caps.

I was fortunate to be born into a family passionate about sport and especially cricket – well, that is apart from my late long – suffering mother and younger sister.

My dad and older brother stuck a bat in my hand and then berated me for many a year because I decided to bat left-handed even though I did everything else right-handed.

At Crowfoot Primary School in Beccles, teacher Brian Patrick got us youngsters playing with a soft ball in the early 1950s but it was when at age 11 I arrived at The Sir John Leman School in the town that the great days began.

Derek Moore batting

David Stewart, a Scot from Stirling, was our sports master. He was also club captain at Lowestoft Cricket Club - and what a coach he was! I was lucky enough to play in the school first team alongside Douglas Mattocks (later to be an outstanding Norfolk wicketkeeper) and Trevor Westwood, who as an 18-year-old fast bowler was already opening the attack for Suffolk in the Minor Counties. With three other pacemen in the team who all went on to play senior club cricket my ambitions as a Laker-like off spinner were totally destroyed. I bowled just one over in two seasons.

I remember when we played Yarmouth Grammar School and after posting something over 150 we (Westwood) demolished the opposition for 5. Westwood finished with 8 for 2 and really the game should have been stopped for cruelty to minors. Remember, there were no helmets then and most boys didn't own a box.

My first game in grown-up cricket was for Beccles A against Loddon aged about 14. I was horrified to be asked to open the batting but made a creditable 14 before being bowled by David Pearce.

I continued to pose as an opening batsman for most of my cricketing life and although I preferred fielding at slip, gully or short-leg I did keep wicket quite a bit.

I eventually moved to Lowestoft Cricket Club which was considered THE place to be if you played in North Suffolk. The Denes Oval was a bowler's graveyard in those days. The pitch was so smooth and flat that even a forward defensive shot would whistle to the boundary if no fielder barred its trajectory. We were spoilt and sometimes struggled on lesser pitches in the wilds of the Norfolk circuit. Incidentally all North Suffolk clubs played mainly in Norfolk. Suffolk CC and clubs south of Halesworth did not seem to know we existed.

It was at Lowestoft that I realised I had to concentrate on close fielding after being humiliated about my lack of any sort of throwing ability.

In the A team there was a rotund chap called Charlie Bowman who after winding up his arm furiously could throw about 10 yards. Thereafter whenever a throw came in to the keeper the call would go out "Well thrown – 15 Charlies". My moment of humiliation was complete when hurling the ball in from fine leg some wag called "half a Charlie."

I worked at Birds Eye in the 1960s and our evening sides played regularly in the Yarmouth Coronation Cup. One year we progressed to the semi-finals and I had one hell of a dilemma.

I opened the batting and had been getting a few runs in the competition and the team was relying on me to be there for this "big game". The problem was I was also singing in a rock band called the Blackjacks and we were on at the Garibaldi on the same evening at 7.30. The captain urged me to turn up and hope we won the toss. We didn't and fielded first against a very strong Gorleston side.

Birds Eye Lowestoft Cricket Club - Winners of the Yarmouth Coronation Cup in 1964

When we came to bat I reckoned I had got eight overs and then I would have to go or risk being late on the stage. With John Cullen and Kenny Smithson bowling pretty quickly and accurately I decided to throw the bat at every ball in the hope I might get a few but also get out and carry on trying to become a pop star. So there I was hoicking, lofting and actually playing a few real shots and after eight overs we were 70 plus for no wicket and I was on 41.

I decided that I had to leave – and so retired. If David Stewart had been there he would have had me publicly flogged. We won the game and went on to win the cup. I wonder if my cricketing career would have been more glorious if I had batted that way all the time. Next day family and friends were calling me up convinced I must be ill or injured having read in the *Evening News* that we had won but D. Moore scored 41 retired. They knew it was just not in my nature to walk off.

I recall a game at Dereham who had a man of the cloth, the Rev. Claude Rutter. He was struggling against our attack and after playing and missing a few times he glanced at the heavens and uttered a pleading "Come on!" Later he stroked a glorious cover drive to the boundary and then looked skywards exclaiming "Thank you!" What a man!

As my cricketing life progressed I found myself playing for a rejuvenated Beccles in the now very competitive Carter Cup 60 overs a side game staring at 11am. This was really posh cricket and we were drawn against Ingham. Now I had been to Ingham many times with Lowestoft and indeed Beccles. It was like going to visit royalty in those days.

Although a tiny village near Stalham, Ingham was the Manchester United of Norfolk cricket. You would always get a generous welcome from dear Jack Borrett, father of the club, and then you would stand in awe as the players arrived. I have been a Norwich City supporter all my days, so imagine how I felt when first Sandy Kennon and then Terry "The Count" Allcock arrived. What joy to be able to listen to these guys in the bar afterwards. There was also a myriad of other top Norfolk players there.

Ingham had the shortest boundaries of any ground I have ever seen. Most fast bowlers started their run with their backside against the boundary fence or adopted a curving start so tight was the space. Everything missed by the wicketkeeper was four byes and I remember keeping to Bernard Haverson of Lowestoft when I was only 10 yards in from the boundary. I swear I once saw somebody leg glance a six which travelled to the boundary no more than six inches above the grass.

Getting back to that Carter Cup tie, I remember walking out to bat at 11am and looking up the pitch to see Tracey Moore standing at the end of his run-up like a Spanish bull just about to duff up the matador. It was at this moment I suddenly but unhelpfully recalled that the day before Tracey had been playing for Minor Counties against Yorkshire. He had taken five wickets including Boycott – so what the hell was I doing there?

On the attack - Tracey Moore shone as a bowler for Ingham and Norfolk.

Now you know cricketers do not wear brown trousers. We had a box but no helmets and I merely had my cap tucked in my pocket facing the ball as a sort of extra padding. The first ball delivery came like a thunderbolt hitting me in the middle of my chest. I later found a seam mark imprinted in the skin which lasted a week. Tracey just grinned gently saying "Welcome to Ingham, Derek".

Next ball I made the fatal mistake of sending what I thought was the most perfect cover drive to the boundary for four. In fact, I never set eyes on it. I just remember that awful sound of falling timber. I didn't look round but just went and hid in a darkened dressing room. It was mostly like that at Ingham. How much did we suffer, I wonder, simply because we were in awe of that club and its famous names?

Many top Norfolk sides in those days were village clubs. Bradfield put out a very strong side and I seem to remember you could see seven church towers as you looked around the field after taking guard. Horsford was very much a village side with its plethora of Wilkinsons long before becoming the Norfolk County headquarters after Lakenham...

My earliest memories include matches at Hales Green near Loddon where soccer was also played in winter. The pitch was not too bad but you were conscious of ruining your wedding potential when going on the front foot. Hales were a genuine village side with most of their players living locally.

It is probably worth considering cricket today against what went on in our youth. You would be lucky to have two umpires with players having to chip in to ensure a game went on. Most knew some of the rules and a whole team might know 90 per cent but common sense and a need to get to the bar ensued their were few arguments. Players rarely questioned a decision on the field.

I can only recall two difficult moments, both involving Bernard Haverson, a very fast and effective bowler. While playing for Lowestoft at Ingham, Bernard felled Cyril Adams, the home wicketkeeper, who lay groaning on the pitch. Both sides were concerned and gathered around the prostrate figure – all except Bernard who shouted his insistence to get him on his feet or get him off – truly a real fast bowler's sentiments. On another occasion while playing for Beccles against Norwich Wanderers, Bernard whipped off the bails at the end of his explosive run-up because David Pilch, a gentleman by birth and Norfolk captain, was backing up out of his crease. Despite appeals by his own side Bernard insisted that he had to go and the umpire was left with no alternative. It caused some bad feeling but Bernard was adamant it was cheating .... And he never quite liked public schoolboys.

Oh yes, another incident worth mentioning. Beccles batsman Bob Scales played a defensive shot and without a thought tapped the ball back to the bowler with a second contact. A Yorkshireman bowling for Overstrand at the time appealed for "hit the ball twice" and Bob was on his way. What a pity I cannot remember the bowler's name but the fact he was from Yorkshire says it all.

There are a quite a few things about modern club cricket I find hard to accept: I am horrified to hear that even junior clubs have a so-called professional. Usually a youngster from abroad with some dubious pedigree which struggles to be repeated in the East Anglian climate. These guys get paid substantial sums – yes get paid. The rest pay a portion of their hard-earned wages to be part of the team. This cannot be good for cricket long term. Surely better to have a promising youngster in the side than a ringer soaking up club funds?

Now cricket at all levels seems to be the mirror image of the big game, even aping the glitzy and exciting form of the Coronation Cup called the Indian Premier League.

While at Beccles a year or two ago for a Vice-Presidents' lunch I noted a lot of young men in matching track suits and baseball caps jogging around the pitch. "Who are they?" I asked my brother John. "That's the first eleven warming up" he said, seeming surprised I had asked. I said we used to warm up in the bar... "Are they any good?" I asked John and George Slater, another stalwart of Beccles and Yarmouth. "Not half as good as we were" they replied. I watched the game and they were right.

I played my last game aged 55 and retired hurriedly when my son insisted I was lapped on a single. He later posted a note on my cricket bag reiterating the sentiments of John McEnroe; "The older I get the more I realise how good I used to be". The note is still on that bag and it is still packed.

My bat is under the bed. My son Jeremy asked why. I replied that it might come in handy if I have to confront an intruder. Jeremy's mocking reply was "What's the point? You will only edge him for four".

WHOLESOME FUN

4 August 1860 - Went to a 3 o'clock luncheon-dinner at Captain Haggard's. At the head of the table was a peacock. We played a game of cricket afterwards, the Squire, myself and the menservants all joining in; it is a wholesome English pastime.

Rev Benjamin Armstrong *(A Norfolk Diary)*

TEN

HOBBS THE MASTER

Old Buckenham's picturesque cricket ground, a few miles from Attleborough, was the venue back in 1921 for an unofficial Test Match between England and Australia as an immigrant squire indulged his passion for the game.

Rain and bad light ruled out any chance of a result but time has not dimmed the brilliance of an innings from the batsman many regard as the finest ever to go to the crease.

Jack Hobbs, the poor man's son from Cambridge who became the first professional games player to be knighted, took 85 peerless runs off an intimidating attack on a difficult track before he pulled a thigh muscle and had to retire.

"The Master" failing to reach three-figures was an event in itself – he scored nearly 200 centuries on the first-class beat – but his style and command on the second day of that memorable occasion led him later to vote it the best knock of his career. "Everything went right that day and my strokes came easily" was his own typically modest postscript.

Warwick Armstrong, the beefy Australian captain, considered it as fine as any played for or against his side on that visit. Such magnanimity could have been prompted by the fact that Hobbs did not face the tourists again that summer.

He recovered sufficiently to be selected for the Third Test at Headingley, but had to leave the field with acute stomach pains on the first afternoon. Appendicitis put him out for the rest of the season.

The *Eastern Daily Press* summary of a masterpiece on May 5, 1921, read: "Hobbs gave a splendid display of sound batsmanship, the ease and elegance of his strokes winning admiration and applause. We saw England's great batsman at his best, his driving, cutting and placing being delightful to watch."

The Old Buckenham showpiece was seen as a full dress rehearsal for the real Tests. Only a few months earlier the Aussies drubbed England 5-0 down under. Without Hobbs, England were no match at home either and lost the series 3-0 as fast bowlers Jack Gregory and Ted McDonald ruled the roost.

So what brought Hobbs and many other golden names of cricket to this little corner of Norfolk?

Lionel Robinson, an Australian determined to wear the garb of an English gentleman, found his perfect country seat at Old Buckenham in 1906. He built a palatial hall with 14 bathrooms, adding splendid stables for his racing stud and a cricket ground in a clearing in the wood that surrounded his new home.

He appointed as his personal cricket manager the former England batsman Archie MacLaren, who lived in a cottage on the estate for many years. Special turf was imported from Australia to improve the pitch... and it seemed a good idea to invite a few of the "local boys" to try it out.

The Australians agreed to play the second match of their tour at Old Buckenham in the first week of May, 1921. It became billed as "The Private Test Match" and about 2000 cricket lovers filed into the ground on May 4, the first day. The EDP reported: "There was a great pilgrimage from all parts of Norfolk and the adjoining counties, and as the

Lionel Robinson with the Australians at Old Buckenham in 1921.

road traffic drew nearer the magnetic centre, the country folk, all wide-eyed, no doubt wondered that a mere cricket match could cause so much commotion and stir... Never before had so many enthusiasts come from near and far."

The weather refused to play ball. Rain lashed down and only 15 minutes of play was possible. The EDP included this gem: "A facetious person said that an Australian match should be substitute for the customary prayer for rain and the farmers would be on a winner every time!"

This was an obvious reference to the last occasion the Australians had played in Norfolk in 1912. Norwich became isolated from the outside world by floods and other areas were devastated after record downpours.

A welcome sun presided over the second day as if in anticipation of riches to come. From early morning all roads in the area were under siege. Estimates of the crowd varies between 7000 and 10,000. The EDP correspondent waxed lyrical:

"This was one of the most wonderful days in the history of Norfolk cricket... Ranged behind the deep human wall were hundreds upon hundreds of motor cars, the roofs of which were converted into stands, and from these lofty perches distant view were obtained of the play. The park trees, now in their May glory of leaf, alone were sacred..."

The Australians were bowled out for 136 an hour after lunch, their lowest total of the tour. The English reply was built round Hobbs and his undoubted class. Sadly, the rain returned to mock the chances of a morale-boosting home win.

The third and final day was drab, damp and sunless, but talk of Hobbs at his peak helped dispel some of the gloom. "To Norfolk the fixture has been a great and memorable event and the incidents of the match will be the gossip of the countryside and cricket pavilions for years to come" said the EDP with pardonable relish.

Lionel Robinson died the following year and was buried outside the north door of the thatched village church. Old Buckenham Hall became a boys' school but fire ravaged the building in the early 1950s. The school moved to Brettenham in Suffolk, taking Robinson's beloved thatched cricket pavilion with it.

Old Buckenham Cricket Club were invited to move from the village green to the famous but near derelict ground in the 1960s, gradually restoring it to its old splendour. I made a few visits with my Caister colleagues for league, cup and friendly fixtures. I always found it hard to concentrate at third man or wherever it was deemed I would be in least danger of being asked to influence proceedings.

Groundsman Billy Lancaster told stirring yarns of the Australian end. "You've come down the Road to Paradise" he reminded me one Sunday afternoon as the trees whispered timeless tales of thousands of spectators watching The Master at work on a sunny May day.

I listened intently and heard John Arlott, the Voice of Summer, put glorious action into suitable words... "Others scored faster, hit the ball harder, more obviously murdered bowling; no-one else, though, ever batted with more consummate skill than Jack Hobbs."

And he saved his best for Norfolk.

OTHER NORFOLK VISITS

Hobbs put his blossoming skills on display against Norfolk in 1904.

He spent two summers qualifying for Surrey and found top form during the second when he was "put out to grass" with Cambridgeshire. After scores of 54 and 52 against Oxfordshire, he heard Surrey were having him watched in the next game, with Norfolk and Norwich.

Hobbs made 92 in two and a half hours. That helped Surrey fully to recognise his outstanding talents at the crease. Basil Cozens-Hardy, one of the bowlers to suffer, maintained that the number of legside boundaries he conceded won Jack Hobbs his Surrey place.

A couple of years after his vintage display against the Australians at Old Buckenham, Hobbs was back in Norfolk, this time to open the cricket nets for the YMCA at St Giles in Norwich. Harold Theobald, Jack Read and R G Pilch snr, were among Norfolk players who bowled to Hobbs in front of a small crowd.

Hobbs scored 61,237 first class runs, including 197 centuries, between 1905 and 1934. He scored at least one century in every English season and on every tour. He scored hundreds against every English county, both Universities, MCC, the three countries against whom he played Tests – Australia, South Africa and West Indies – for Players' v Gentlemen and for Rest v Champion County.

He was knighted in 1953. He died in Hove in 1963.

OLD BUCKENHAM SCOREBOARD

AUSTRALIANS

First innings

W Bardsley	c White	b Douglas	10
H L Collins	c Knight	b Gibson	23
C G Macartney	c Wood	b Douglas	11
J M Taylor	run-out		20
W Armstrong	not out		51
J M Gregory	lbw	Douglas	2
J S Ryder	c Knight	b Douglas	0
E L Hendry	c Chapman	b Gibson	5
H Carter	c Jupp	b Gibson	2
E A McDonald	lbw	Douglas	0
A A Mailey	lbw	Douglas	4
Extras			8
Total			136

Bowling:
Douglas 22.5 – 6 – 64 – 6,
Jupp 2 – 0 – 19 – 0,
Gibson 16 – 3 – 33 – 3,
White 4 – 2 – 12 – 0

Second Innings

W.Bardsley	not out		8
H L Collins	c Fender	b Gibson	15
C G Macartney	not out		1
Extra			1
Total (1 wkt)			25

Bowling:
Douglas 5 – 1 – 15 – 0,
Gibson 9 – 8 – 1 – 1,
White 4 – 2 – 12 – 0

PARSON THROUGH

The *Eastern Daily Press* reported in July, 1893:
A clergyman by the name of Bishop was batting in a local cricket match. On the bowler sending him a very wide ball he cried out; "Keep the ball in the parish, sir!"

The very next ball took his middle stump whereon the bowler remarked; "I think that's about the diocese, my lord."

ENGLAND XI

First Innings

D J Knight	lbw McDonald		1
J Hobbs	retired hurt		85
V W C Jupp	retired hurt		59
P Hendren	c Hendry	b McDonald	20
A P F Chapman	c Hendry	b McDonald	0
J W H T Douglas	not out		41
P G H Fender	c Hendry	b McDonald	10
G E C Wood	c Gregory	b Hendry	2
C H Gibson	c Mailey	b Gregory	1
J C White	b Gregory		0
A C MacLaren	not out		25
Extras			25
Total (7 wkts dec)			256

Bowling:
Gregory 13 – 1 – 45 – 2,
McDonald 25 – 4 – 62 – 4,
Macartney 6 – 1 – 18 – 0,
Hendry 30 – 10 – 73 – 1,
Mailey 6 – 0 – 46 – 0

ELEVEN

OUT OF THE ASHES

Tom Walshe lived in Old Buckenham as a small child where his grandfather ran a village shop and garage. He started playing cricket at Thetford Grammar School and captained the school first XI in 1968. He was a resident of Attleborough for 30 years, and helped re-establish the town's cricket team in the mid-1960s. When the club folded again in 1974, he joined Old Buckenham where he played for nearly 10 years, became club captain and was later found an even more useful role as chairman. As a local journalist, he has reported on cricket and written about characters involved in the game.

Here he traces the return of cricket to Old Buckenham Hall in the 1960s following a disastrous fire that had reduced the scene of an unofficial Ashes match to ashes and dereliction, and recalls characters who brought life and laughter to the lovely ground's renaissance years

If there is an Elysian field where cricket is played in Norfolk, then perhaps it is at Old Buckenham Hall. Carved from a woodland fringe during the golden age of country house cricket, the ground is a spiritual home to many who love the game. Its remarkable history almost seems to echo from the enclosing trees.

Jack Hobbs sat there, beneath the branches of a mighty beech and, out in the sunny middle on May 5th 1921, fashioned what he later described as his greatest innings. Another England legend, Archie MacLaren, often strolled up the woodland track from The Manor, his grace-and-favour home as cricket manager on Lionel Robinson's estate. And on the square, he tossed a coin with Australia's colossal captain, Warwick

Armstrong, to signal the start of the most illustrious match ever played in the county.

The scenery has altered somewhat since England and Australia's finest met at Old Buckenham Hall all those years ago. But, as a cricket theatre, it is still as captivating. Gone is most of the vast house that Robinson, a Mr. Moneybags from Melbourne, erected in a brash statement of his wealth and sporting patronage. The building burned down in 1952 after becoming home to one of East Anglia's leading prep schools.

Gone too – removed to Brettenham in Suffolk, along with the school – is the rustic thatched pavilion where gentlemen cricketers enjoyed lavish lunches, attended by a butler and liveried footmen. And gone is the massive three-centuries-old beech that gave generous shade to Hobbs and hundreds more, blighted by disease in its old age towards the millennium's close.

Today a smart and spacious brick clubhouse and impressive scoreboard mark the progress of the village team and its prominence in the Norfolk Cricket Alliance. The boundary is defined by advertising boards reflecting the commercial realities of the 21st century. New practice nets, paid for by European Union funding, sit pristinely near the site of the old thatched pavilion. No fewer than nine teams flourish now under the banner of Old Buckenham CC, including those catering for young and not-so-young as well as, praise be, a girls' eleven.

Many people have contributed to the success of cricket at the hall over the last 50 years, none more so than the current group of players and officials. But the glue that has really held it together has been supplied by the Panks family, with the pivotal roles filled by twin brothers Horace and William – more familiarly known in Norfolk cricket circles as Horry and Will.

The Panks are to Old Buckenham what the Archers are to Ambridge. Four generations – female as well as male – have played their roles in this everyday story of cricket folk. These days Horry is club president, chief groundsman and father figure. Will serves behind the clubhouse bar.

But let's rewind to the late 1950s. Robinson's lovely ground had become overgrown and neglected, scarcely recognisable as a cricket arena. Insult was added to its injury by a motor cycle grass track scarring the perimeter.

The Panks boys, small but lithe and strong and near identical, and their father Ernie were in the vanguard of its renaissance. As a farmer whose land bordered the hall grounds, Ernie cut a summer crop of hay from the old cricket field. Oliver and Greeba Sear were the new owners, having made their home in an annexe of the hall that survived the fire.

Twins Will (left) and Horry Panks meet England all-rounder Trevor Bailey at Norwich Lads' Club in 1956. Looking on (left) is Norfolk legend Michael Falcon, who often played at Old Buckenham in Lionel Robinson's era.

Motor racing was Oliver's sport, not cricket, and he was one of the founders of the Snetterton circuit. However, he had a sense of history and believed in encouraging local enterprise so, when Ernie Panks remarked to him one day, "Wouldn't it be nice to see cricket at the hall again?" he immediately replied, "If you'll do the work, you can play here."

The very next day, a group led by Ernie and the teenaged twins, along with village team captain, Billy Lancaster, set about the task of reclaiming the ground for cricket.

Village lads had never had much opportunity to play at the hall. In its first five decades it had been primarily the province of gentlemen and scholars, while the village club's home pitches were various fields around the parish and, latterly, a concrete-and-matting strip on the village green. But all that changed when, for the 1961 season, they left behind the concrete pitch (along with the prohibition of Sunday fixtures in deference to chapel folk) and moved up to the hall.

In those days Old Buckenham had the classic blend of experience and youth. Billy Lancaster was the experience; most of the rest were the youth. "If Billy got 40 or 50, the team might get to 80," Horry recalls. "If he didn't, we were struggling." Buckenham had some good young bowlers though. Horry, fast left-arm, opened the attack; at the other end were Billy Hales or Eddie Cocking.

Low scores were the norm in those days when wickets were often ill-prepared and subject to the vagaries of the weather. Many away grounds doubled as farmers' fields and often the cows or sheep had to be rounded up before play began. "In the early 1960s we'd often go home with cow-muck on our whites, and we'd have a job persuading mother that we'd been playing cricket." says Horry.

One such venue was Pulham where the offending dung had to be swept from the wicket before play began. It left a residue that caused the ball to skid through, or fizz off a length. Panks and Hales ran through Pulham and bowled them out for 14. An Old Buckenham victory appeared a formality, but Lancaster cautioned: "Dorn't yew be tew cocky – they ha' got thar buggers (i.e. the runs)." Sure enough, Old Buckenham were also dismissed for 14.

At Cressingham, the bovine effects were counteracted by a mat laid on the wicket. It didn't make batting any easier. Buckenham went in and got 41 before Eddie Cocking wiped the floor with the home team who were all out for 10.

Horry took 100 wickets in a season for the first time at the age of 16, and was regularly top of the averages with 90 or more wickets. His last ton-up haul was in 1975, Old Buckenham's first year in league cricket, and no-one has achieved the feat since.

Old Buckenham face the camera in 1975 - Tom Walshe is in the middle of the front row .

As a swing bowler, particularly when atmospheric conditions were favourable, HP had few peers in the local game. A prodigious talent, he played for Attleborough on Sundays because of the Lord's Day observance imposed by Old Buckenham's grandees. These days he might well have been considered for county honours.

Attleborough had one of the best club sides in Norfolk in the 1950s and early 60s when Fred Barnard (known as "Dealer" or "Bish", sports shop proprietor and a real Mr Cricket of the post-war era) put together a formidable team drawn largely from staff at Wymondham College and those locals he deemed talented enough to be invited to play.

My own appetite for cricket was whetted when, as a 10-year-old in 1960, I would sit on an old cast-iron roller at Attleborough Recreation Ground to while away spellbound Sunday afternoons watching young Horry steaming in to bowl. And, when Attleborough batted, there was beefy, bespectacled opening bat Keith Rutherford smiting sixes above my head into the trees. Or, as shadows lengthened in the evening sun, the Dealer himself winkling out the opposition with his mesmerising spinners.

I recall a match against a touring side called Palmer's School when Attleborough's Charlie Lawrence (who during the week blew the hooter that signalled the start and end of the working day at Gaymers' cider factory) sent the locals home happy by hitting the last ball for six to win the game.

A few years later, after some of the Dealer's transient friends departed, a group of us youngsters, aided by old hands such as Lawrence, Bob Myhill and Roy Melton, kept cricket going at Attleborough for a few more years until the football club won the battle for space on "the Rec." and some of our best young players had gone off to university. Bob

Myhill's son Neil, Chris Allen, Geoff Batley, Doug Chenery, Dave Philpot, Ian Winter and I were among Attleborough exiles who found our way to Old Buckenham.

The hall ground in the 1970s was, as it is today, a wonderful place to play, but other facilities were non-existent. There was no pavilion and no loos: we changed two miles away at the Crown pub beside the village green (now the Ox and Plough), dashed back there by car for teas and toilets, and later re-lived the day's play over copious pints while squashed noisily into the public bar.

One voice was always unmistakable both on the field and in the pub. Billy Lancaster, club captain and chief groundsman, was a fine cricketer and a gem of a character. An attack of mumps in adulthood had left his features slightly skewhiff, and he talked with a Norfolk drawl from the side of his mouth. But he spoke good cricket sense.

In his youth he was a quick bowler and swashbuckling batsman. Later he switched to being a wily spinner and remained a valued member of Old Buckenham's bowling attack into his mid-50s, though by that time we sometimes feared for his life when, anchored at first slip, he failed to sight the edged catch that whistled past his spectacles to the boundary. "Di'nt see it in the trees," he would announce in his raucous tones, more by way of excuse than apology. No one was more surprised than Bill when one day he stuck out an involuntary hand and clung on to one that looked about to take off his ear.

He knew every blade of grass on the Old Buckenham square. The "Australian end" (on the wooded side) was the place to play, he assured us all, where soil imported by Lionel Robinson from Down Under to create a fast and true wicket retained its effect.

Bill could be a bit tetchy on a bad day and, if there was one person guaranteed to wind him up, it was club secretary, Derek Hardy. It wasn't intentional, let's just say that both were strong-willed and stubborn and had their own ideas about how things should be done. Bill certainly would not tolerate any interference or criticism of the wicket from Derek who was periodically banned from setting foot there while Bill was at work.

Having said that, and to paraphrase Nelson, every ship should have a Hardy. He'd never played the game, but was crazy about it. He put in countless hours of fixture arranging, paperwork, telephoning and often did the scoring on match days. As a professional meteorologist, his weather predictions were invaluable, even to the point that, when conditions were favourable and the moles were active, he would sit for hours at the cricket ground waiting to bash the troublesome animals on the

Guard of honour for Billy Lancaster in a special match to mark his 40 years with Old Buckenham.

nose with a hammer as they pushed up their unsightly mounds on the outfield.

To the surprised delight of everyone who suspected he was a born misogynist, Derek eventually found a partner for a long innings, and married work colleague Wendy who is just as mad about cricket and an equally efficient scorer. Together they migrated with the Met. Office down to Devon where both are now giving sterling service to Chudleigh Cricket Club.

Another great clubman of that era was Roger Macrow, a gentle giant of 21 stone who, while not the most gifted cricketer, was a handy chap to have around whenever anything needed lifting, pinning down...or eating. Roger cut an imposing figure at short leg, where he usually fielded on the basis that running was not his strong suit and the batsman's scoring options were restricted by his bulky presence.

One day, having over-indulged on blackcurrant tart at lunch, he suddenly asked permission to leave the field for a toilet break in the woods. Few had seen Roger move quite so quickly but, alas, not quite quickly enough. On emerging from the trees, he requested to be allowed to remain in the outfield for the rest of the innings... where the stain on the back of his flannels would not be so apparent.

Roger's weighty reputation went before him. Deopham cricketers quaintly had a rather dilapidated double-decker bus as their changing rooms, with the visitors allotted the upper deck. Legend has it that Roger was asked not to change upstairs in case he compromised the vehicle's structural integrity.

He was a lovely man and a great supporter of the club, so his sudden death aged just 49 was a big shock. A timely reminder of his contribution is to be found in the form of a pavilion clock bearing his name. Its round face always reminds me of Roger's own rotund but friendly visage.

Inevitably life's innings has been cut short for other good friends over the years and a memorial garden next to the clubhouse commemorates one in particular, Angela Panks, wife of Horry and a tireless worker for OBCC. Not only was Angela one of those essential assets to any cricket club, a tea lady, she helped raise thousands of pounds through the social committee and was ex-officio in many other capacities as Horry's right-hand woman.

In another example of service to the cricket club, she and Horry produced daughter Mandy who became an accomplished scorer and occasional player. Now Mandy's own daughter, Francesca Welham, regularly turns out for the girls' team, as the fourth generation Panks to make her mark. It's been a family journey for Will Panks as well: his wife Marjorie and sons Ernest and Malcolm have all been involved with Old Buckenham cricket, on and off the field.

The 1970s saw the arrival of new players as the cricket became more serious and competitive. Old Buckenham joined the Norfolk League in 1975, quickly progressing from the third to the first division. One of the most significant recruits was Yorkshireman John Lund, a teacher at Attleborough High School, in whom we found just the man to inject some steel into the team. Sometimes the steel was a little too tough for those not used to the no-nonsense approach derived from his Boycott-style cricket apprenticeship, but there was seldom a dull moment with John in the side. Swardeston tempted him away for a while, but he's been back at Bucks for some time, is club chairman and still playing almost 40 years on from his debut.

Most people have a cricket tale about Lundy. Here's mine. We were playing Jentique in a league match at Dereham in 1976. John had arranged a flight back from a holiday in Yugoslavia (as it then was) on the morning of the match, and had assured secretary Derek Hardy that he'd be there. In the interim, however, Derek was alarmed to hear that an air traffic controllers' strike was set to delay flights from the continent. Convinced that John wouldn't make it, Derek decided not to put his name forward for inclusion.

Naturally, a few minutes before the start of play, John's car steamed into the ground. Soon the air was turning blue and fumes rising into the Norfolk sky as he reflected on what appeared to be a fruitless 2000-mile dash. In fairness to the Hon. Sec., there had been no communication to say he was on course (no mobile phones or email then, of course). As captain, I decided to defuse the situation by stepping aside. It was an obvious solution – John was the better batsman and his bowling was a big asset to the team...

It was all change again at Old Buckenham in the early 1980s. The club joined the Norfolk Cricket Alliance in 1983. We lost Bill Lancaster to a cruel, debilitating illness. Horry continued as the head groundsman – a role he still fulfils, having now looked after the Old Buckenham wicket for a full 50 years. He also took up umpiring, as did brother Will, the two of them sometimes officiating together at matches all over East Anglia. As in their playing days, cricketers had to look twice to make sure they weren't seeing double.

History continued to be made at the hall as, in 1982, the club secured its future by purchasing the ground. Racehorse breeder and huntsman Tim Finch, who owned the adjacent Winter Paddocks stud, had bought the land from the Sears in the 1970s but was moving to Devon to become Master of the Exmoor Hunt. The club had nothing like the £8500 needed to meet the asking price, and no time to raise the money. However, a great supporter of local sport, Attleborough businessman Eric Winter, came to the rescue by providing an interest-free loan to allow the purchase to go ahead.

As tenants, the club had never been able to erect bricks-and-mortar buildings. Two sectional units provided changing rooms and much-needed toilet facilities for some ten years until the 1987 hurricane proved a wind of change by wrecking the buildings and prompting the ambitious scheme for a permanent brick clubhouse. Within a few months, the £45,000 building cost was met through fund-raising, donations and loans. Messrs Hobbs and MacLaren would have been impressed with the result, I'm sure.

Our friend Keith Skipper once described Old Buckenham's cricket ground as "a little piece of heaven". An apt description. And maybe one that is poignantly fitting with regard to a certain cricketer whose ashes were unofficially and unceremoniously scattered at the ground by his widow, unhappy about a few things that went on in their lives. He, of course, might well have viewed it as a suitable resting place in any case.

If we do get a second innings, let's all hope we can play it somewhere as heavenly as Old Buckenham Hall.

GAPS IN THE FIELD

Norwich City Football Club historian Mike Davage also enjoys digging up unusual cricket stories. This one features former Norwich School prodigy Lt Col Claude Treglown MC, who played 23 times for Norfolk before moving to Essex.

The match in question was Essex v Surrey at Leyton in May, 1925. It ended in a draw. Only two Surrey players, Percy Fender and Alfred Jeacocks, were on the ground for the scheduled start of play, 11.15, on the last morning. The Surrey team bus had been held up in traffic. Fender and Jeacocks had both travelled by car.

Essex captain Johnny Douglas declined to delay start of play, so the two Surrey players took the field with umpires at the appointed time. The two overnight not out Essex batsmen initially failed to appear and only emerged when Fender asked the umpires, Butt and Stone, to remind Douglas of the law - Fender to claim the match if the batsmen did not appear.

The two Essex batsmen, Claude Treglown and Robert Sharp, played four to five overs without scoring off the fielderless bowling of Fender and Jeacocks until the rest of the Surrey team arrived. The overs were not recorded and the scorebook shows no trace of anything unusual.

No newspaper carried a report of the incident as Percy Perrin of Essex argued that any story of the affair would damage the good name of cricket.

The story eventually came to light in Fender's 1981 biography.

Tea interval for hungry cricketers at Snettterton in 1925.

Time for tea at a match between Mastham and a representative team from the rest of the George Beck League in 1938 at Starling's Meadow.

TWELVE

PRESS FOR MEMORIES

I conjured countless match reports out of bare statistics in scorebooks during my reporting years on local newspapers when other duties denied me the pleasure of spending hours with pad and pencil on the boundary. Even so, there were occasional treats as I ploughed cricket furrows at Dereham and Yarmouth before taking up residence on the sports desk in Norwich. As regular columnist in the Eastern Daily Press *for the best part of 30 years, I have turned to the summer game for renewed inspiration. Here are a few favourite innings from the files.*

THE OTHER PARFITT... JULY, 1987

Songs of Praise at Foxley Parish Church started the cricket ball rolling –and we hadn't even been treated to the story of those fishermen chaps who toiled in the deep and caught nothing.

Pardon my mild irreverence. It's just that I knew the great summer game would demand a little outing as soon as I saw John Parfitt in the congregation.

Singing gave way to mardling over a cup of coffee just behind the boundary line at St Thomas' Church. John has long accepted that any chat about cricket will lead invariably to inquiries about Peter, the brother who made such durable marks with Norfolk, Middlesex and England.

Even so, I managed to veer from the orthodox line and reminded John that I'd seen much more of his batting career when I was a young reporter on the Dereham and Fakenham Times. Perhaps the fact I have four brothers whose sporting pedigrees put me in the shade has nurtured a sympathetic streak.

We rolled back the years and announced names as if all his old colleagues were filing through the village church door on a balmy July evening. Walter Brand, George Mason, Cecil Cook, Derek Chamberlain, Freddie Masters, Claude Rutter, the cricketing parson ... and several more Dereham Town stalwarts from the 1960s.

My immediate reward for joining John in local pastures green was a delightful true story to add to my collection. It came from his father's funeral at Foxley Church. They didn't think many would want to carry on to the crematorium but several of Alec Parfitt's old cricketing colleagues were eager to make the journey.

They piled into the motors and were well on their way when one of them noticed the parson was missing.

"Hey, John, bor ... suffin here your dad wunt like." John was perplexed. "Woss that, then?" Back came the answer: "Wuh, yew know he wunt never go to a match wi'owt an umpire!"

From St Thomas to Sir Geoffrey. Well, some of his supporters address him thus. Some critics have conferred less flattering titles on Boycott, the master batsman although I tend to think he does not mind as long as he's being noticed.

He came among us to promote his autobiography with a few choice words for the Yorkshire committee and the odd reprimand for anyone who might have crossed him during a prolific stint at the crease.

On the whole, however, I found him much more amenable than on our previous meeting in September, 1980. On that occasion he was presenting an illustrated lecture in Norwich. He granted me an audience before the show and agreed to record a "Welcome BBC Radio Norfolk" message. The station was opening the following day and I rather fancied a world exclusive to go with the fanfare.

Boycott's little eulogy based firmly on "my old opening partner from Norfolk, John Edrich" dried dramatically when I found the temerity to pose a question about the latest round of the civil war at Yorkshire.

"You've no right to ask me questions like that, young man" he growled, chucking in an expletive or three. The interview was over ....to be resumed in July, 1987, on a much more placid wicket. Geoffrey met all deliveries with a measured smile.

I proved I'd read his words carefully by proclaiming gleefully that a Norfolk lad seemed to be responsible for the nickname he collected during the fifth Test against South Africa at Port Elizabeth in 1965. Eddie Barlow was caught at slip off Boycott's bowling by ... Peter Parfitt!

"I might not be as good a slipper as Sharpey but I got that one, Fiery!"shouted Parfitt. Boycott says; "I came to realise I had a new nickname which was likely to stick. I have since heard lots of stories about the nickname Fiery. Many people have naturally insisted that it is an ironic reference to my speed and demeanour with the bat!

"But the name first came into currency on that South African tour and was derived from the fact that Fred Trueman was Fiery Fred to the public and just about every headline writer in the newspapers. It followed that since I was from Yorkshire I would be GeofFiery – and the name was shortened to Fiery when Fred was no longer on the England scene."

Be honest, it would take a shrewd Norfolk brain made in Billingford and sharpened at Fakenham Grammar School to come up with something like that.

Alborough line up of 1955.

Bradenham's ground in the early 1960s. George Mason is batting for Dereham.

OMINOUS CLOUDS... AUGUST, 1997

If sport and all the trimmings truly mirror our society, I am sorely tempted to buy a one-way ticket to Botany Bay.

England's abject surrender at Trent Bridge ought to provide more than another ritual sackcloth-and-ashes session for cricket's hierarchy. The backcloth against which this latest humiliation was played out must force those who run the game to note ominous clouds overhead.

Test matches remain special occasions despite England's recent proclivity for defeat. I went to Nottingham in hope. I left in despair, not all of it based on the sight of Aussies in a triumphant mid-pitch huddle as the last wicket fell.

I sat with two cricket-loving friends in the William Clarke Stand, named after the underarm bowling wizard who turned a meadow into a ground destined to become one of the game's most famous international stages.

I suspect spectators in early Victorian times gave occasional vent to their feelings and sampled various forms of refreshment as contests unfolded in unbroken sunshine. But how on earth did they manage without a portable fridge? Or the Barmy Army Songbook?

Chanting, yelling, posturing and drinking wrapped up in the latest replica soccer shirt dominated a day so far removed from the world of cricket I knew and admired as a boy. Laddish groups, mostly oblivious to folk of all ages around them, kept up a grubby cacophony hijacked from football's terraces. Decibel levels rose with the temperature and a worsening of England's plight.

Stewards and police moved in eventually after letting it boil up into an anti-social lather, histrionics fuelled by unlimited access to alcohol and instant replays of key incidents on giant screens.

A whiff of hypocrisy surrounded a spate of late-afternoon ejections and I couldn't help wondering if law and order forces would have dared take action at all had the contest been of a more equal nature out in the middle.

There was also the strange business over a small Union Flag. A young man was told not to wave it by stewards who then mocked their own strictures by ignoring a young man brandishing an Australian flag a few rows away.

As baying and insulting drowned the chance of any reasonable debate on patriotism, I thought of a packed Mundesley Coronation Hall the night before as the local festival reached a rousing climax on the Norfolk coast.

We cheered and proudly unfurled our flags at this homely version of Last Night of the Proms. Trent Bridge was awash with jeers, boos and boorish behaviour to accompany the Fast Flight of the Poms.

TRENDY CULTURE – JULY, 2004

I told the wife straight. "I'm off to London with the lads to see glamorous performers in bright pyjamas strip our emotions bare."

She smiled knowingly, packed lunch and avowed younger son would make sure I didn't get lost or confused in the big city.

We caught a bus a little after 6 am and headed for the fleshpots of NW8, arriving as the first catwalk drama unfolded. Trescothick already undone!

Cromer High School's outing to Lord's to watch the one-day cricket international between England and West Indies yielded a memorable run feast and the obligatory cries of "shambles!" and "crisis!" over a home defeat.

We sat, appropriately, on the lower tier of the Edrich Stand, named after buccaneer Bill, the Norfolk, Middlesex and England maestro. I bored younger son with a potted history of one of my sporting heroes. He asked if I preferred a cheese or chicken sandwich.

I fondly recalled my first school trip to see "proper" cricketers, the West Indies tourists taking on Cambridge University at Fenner's. Potted meat sandwiches dominated that blustery day.

My first visit in years to headquarters in the district of St John's Wood, loftier than a suburb but still lowlier than the likes of Mayfair and Belgravia, simply underlined London's hideous traffic problems and cricket's shameless embrace of high-powered commerce and trendy culture.

With blazers, striped ties and panama hats easily outscored by track-suits, trainers and baseball caps, it was more like a pop festival or a tribute to Euro 2004 than a celebration of our great summer game.

Chanting, cheering, stamping and straddling seats as well as more sedate patrons in the hunt for liquid reinforcements, this growing army must intimidate traditionalists who dare to go to cricket matches to watch, clap and gently appreciate.

Then there's the "wag" who selects key moments in the action to air his latest routine, liberally spiced with expletives banned from his local pub. Such ale-and-hearty entertainers are proliferating at an alarming rate.

Fashion accessories piled high in the Lord's shop show exactly where the game has gone, on and off the field, presumably with the full blessing of sartorially-elegant MCC members and other notables in the far pavilions of power.

Just as the beer tent has been superseded by the corporate hospitality box, so will all aspects of our best-loved game continue to change.

And I'll just carry on lamenting from the Good Old Days End.

Still, perfect weather, nearly 600 runs and plenty of sandwiches to share with younger son rendered it a worthwhile return to Lord's. I promised we'll be back when England are ready to reclaim the Ashes.

A SUNDAY AMBLE... JULY, 2008

It took me eight summers to come out of hiding. Even then, I suffered feelings of disloyalty at circling another boundary in another setting in another era.

I added my plaintive voice to a chorus of dismay greeting final overs for Norfolk county cricket at Lakenham in August, 2000. For over a decade I lived next door to this lovely ground, a lung of fresh air in the middle of a city.

From my bedroom window I could see pitch inspections, picnic hampers, glinting thatch, rippling tents, excited youngsters, phlegmatic veterans, reluctant bicycles, brazen cars and floppy hats. Summer unfolded before my eyes as I returned willingly to the arena for sporting refreshment. A gentle hum after the cacophony of Carrow Road not far away.

That window closed on 173 seasons of Norfolk combat as the hosts

Ingham stalwart Andy Seeley shows caution at the crease.

failed to beat Cheshire and earn a visit to Lord's. There was no fairytale ending. A priceless facility fell victim to "spiralling costs". Tradition was trapped lbw – let business win – and sprawling Horsford waited to feel the weight of history.

I haven't been back to Lakenham. Friends with stronger stomachs for "change", "progress" and "new opportunities" tell me it isn't as bad as all that. I suspect they are being kind to the place and to me.

I hadn't paid a visit to Norfolk's "new" headquarters at Manor Park, scarcely a hedge-hop from Norwich International Airport, until a call from one of my Press Gang entertainment chums suggested I take a Sunday amble with a difference after a length sequence of Cromer cliff top expeditions.

Pat Nearney, a former football referee and marathon runner, and current enthusiast for most local sports, reminded me that Norfolk's cricketers were bidding for their fourth trip to Lord's in a dozen years. The weather looked reasonable for their knockout trophy semi-final against Devon at Horsford. Fresh air and exercise would do us good.

He'd pick me up in an hour. Little time in which to consider of an eight-year absence from the county scene.

A cheery woman on the gate asked if either of us qualified for pensioner's concessions. I told her I hadn't been away that long. Devon were batting. A plane flew over deep square-leg to drown out a blossoming debate between two boundary stalwarts about the seemingly unstoppable charge of Twenty 20 cricket. "We were playing that on village greens for nothing but fun when I was a lad...". I nodded my agreement.

My useful reputation for putting names to faces underwent a thorough examination as our walkabout gained pace. Ray Lusted, Peter Thomas, Barry Battelley, David Armstrong, Terry Moore, Tony King, Brian Bird, John Ford, Richard Aldridge, Les King, David Colman, John Parfitt and Eric Craske were just the warm-up boys. Pat started to get his own back for all these little diversions when he bumped into someone he used to work with at Norwich Union. Then an old refereeing colleague.

Devon were all out for 190.

I came fairly clean during the interval when sporting types at Radio Norfolk ushered me into their tent to fill a few minutes with slightly biased chat. Yes, my first visit to Manor Park. Could do with a few more trees and years before any comparisons can be made. A massive five-a-side football competition for youngsters just behind us mocks the occasion and the season. Norfolk ought to mark my "debut" here with a victory.

They failed by 52 runs. Devon go to Lord's on Wednesday, August 6th. My wife will be pleased. That's the date of our silver wedding anniversary and she may have something planned. Not a bad teatime score these days on the marriage test match scene – 25 for 2.

Come on, cut out the whimsy and face up to short-pitched deliveries from the Home Truths End.

Can an old Lakenham lover forget the past and find true happiness at Horsford? I don't think so, but he has to make the best of any new relationship while cricket remains the one true sport worth courting.

I went to Lord's the Thursday before to watch England pile up runs against South Africa. I didn't see anyone I knew. I went to Manor Park, albeit with a hefty nudge, and met numerous old friends out for a Sunday stroll.

Several referred to Lakenham with due affection and reverence.

BAG OF MEMORIES ... JUNE 2010

Howzat for bold individuality! World Cup football in South Africa stealing hearts, hopes and too many hours. So I settle for a calming game of cricket at the tail-end of Victorian Norfolk.

Well, 'tis the season for flannelled fools rather than show-offs in shorts – we love to be disparaging about sport at times of national examination – although dividing lines are too often blurred to know which fashion pitch ought to take priority.

I feel genuine sympathy for talented twin-hatters forced to sacrifice one or the other as fixture lists overlap brazenly enough to suggest that not all men in white coats operate exclusively at Lord's.

"Crazy summers of sport" tend to turn into jingoistic junkets fed by an over-excited media desperate to wave the flag but to waive any semblance of sound judgement. Celebrity pundits rule, okay?

My little local pavilion of solace from the past, lovingly built out of boyhood cricket adventures in the closing overs of the 1800s, was furnished by a major figure in the British theatre. Herbert Farjeon (1887-1945) presented popular revues in London's West End and also relished the roles of critic, lyricist, librettist, playwright, theatre manager and researcher.

His father was the novelist Benjamin Leopold Farjeon. His mother, Margaret Jefferson, was the daughter of American actor Joseph Jefferson. His sister, Eleanor Farjeon, wrote children's verse and stories. His brothers were Harry Farjeon, the composer, and novelist J Jefferson Farjeon. A talented team.

Herbert Farjeon's Cricket Bag, first unpacked in 1946 shortly after his death, remains one of the game's most alluring chronicles knitted together by his brother and fellow enthusiast, J Jefferson, "mixing the nostalgic with the facetious, the correct with reckless play, dividing the game into two innings, with an interval for light refreshment, and closing play with one of his loveliest poems."

A teasing introduction, almost begging the umpire of time to call " play!" again, recalls family holidays on the north Norfolk coast in days when "all red letter-boxes had V.R. on them, and buses were drawn by horses, and war was a mere theory like China and old age, and Arthur Shrewsbury's average was 38.1."

The Farjeon cricket fanatics found their first all-grass pitch in East Runton, opposite Manor Farm, where they were spending eight weeks' summer holiday in 1896. When they became hot and tired, "there, within easy call beyond the duck-pond and the cottage where the old woman of 90 lived, was the sea in which we bathed from little tents, gasping as the first waves reached and enveloped us and then sinking into the lovely coolness up to our necks."

After Runton on one side of Cromer railway station – "one of the loveliest conclusions to a journey in the whole of England" – sporting escapades continued in Trimingham, five miles on the other. A field of rough grass with a few smoothish patches sufficed as a Test arena for three blissful summers.

Trimingham action was not confined to their private bumpy pitch. When the tide withdrew from the base of the high cliffs, passing back over agate-spangled pebbles and pool-haunted gulleys and sliding off smooth stretches beyond, the Farjeon children stuck their stumps in fast-drying sand and collected impromptu teams for tip-and-run.

They even found ways of carrying on in wet weather. "Our farm had an intriguing network of buildings and there were long, covered passages that ran at the back of often-untenanted accommodation for various forms of livestock.

"To this sanctuary when it rained, and when no forbidding livestock was about, Bertie and I would creep, armed with bat and ball and bulls'-eyes to settle in snugly till the weather cleared."

Just to underline how potty about cricket these young visitors were ... "When field, sand and barn all failed, there was still the bedroom passage. Here we played with tennis ball, a hairbrush and a certain unmentionable article of bedroom crockery. If the hairbrush failed to keep the ball out of the bedroom crockery, the batsman was dismissed."

Herbert Farjeon's Cricket Bag, filled to some extent by those golden days in Poppyland, is a perfect antidote to too many raucous alternatives to the real summer game. And, yes, those passionate siblings were worried by the way show-offs in shorts were beginning to dominate over a century ago:

"Papers in September made sad reading. The first football results appeared, edging like an intruding shadow into the final rays of the cricket field. We always felt that football began too early and ended too late, and we noted indignantly how gradually it began earlier and earlier and ended later and later, making the year a thick sandwich with too much bread and not enough butter."

Crumbs, boy Herbert, best you stay clear of the current spread.

THE HAS-BEENS

(excerpt)

We are the good old Has-beens,
As good as good can be,
Tho' getting old and feeble,
Still very good are we.
We're neither young nor handsome,
The girls for us don't crave,
But we shall still play Cricket,
With one foot in the grave.

We can't help missing catches,
Our eyes are not so good,
But we can make excuses,
Just as we always could.
Our Captain he gets furious
The Bowler he says things,
But we'll keep playing Cricket
Till we are sprouting wings.

Lucien Boullemier

THIRTEEN

BUMBLE BOILS

The Norfolk dialect has enjoyed many a good innings when it comes to the local sporting scene. Maurice Woods, a former London editor of the Eastern Daily Press, *wrote Harbert's News from Dumpton in local weekly papers for almost 40 years. Here's his amusing report of the big village opener in Coronation Year, 1953.*

We hed a marster good cricket match larst Saturda, tha fust o' the season. Me, I like cricket. Thass better'n footborl, cos I play. I ent sayin I'm tha best cricketer Dumpton a got, but I carnt think o' no one better orfhand.

Corse, I like footborl tew, but I hatta go as linesman cos thass my best posishun, an thet ent tha searme as bein on tha fild. I reckon they'll hatta give tha linesman's job to somebodda else come next yare, an stick me in at centre-forrard, cos they lorst tha Rewral Districk League Jewbilee Charity Cup this yare, silla lot o' fewls. Them Dedley Resarves won it orf on em, playin dutty like they allers dew, an tha ref wor blind in one eye an coun't see outer tha other.

Howsomever, I ent sorry tha cricket season a come. We're got a hully good side. Bumble, our policeman, he's a good un, leastways he will be when he strike his form. He wor a bit handicapped larst Saturda cos he're got a push. He went to tha doctor, an tha duzzy fewl reckoned thet wor a boil, but thet wornt. Them doctors dornt know narthin.

Corse, I carnt tell yer whare he're got this hare push, but he coun't bend down to dew up his bewt-learces. I hed to dew em up for him. He hent rid his bike neither for a week or more.

✧✧✧

The wicket's in fust-clarss condishun, an yew can say what yew like. The marster a hed his cutter on the medder, an young Rewpert, he're bin a-pullin up tha docks. Me an tha gal Alice, we spent tha best part o' tha Friday evenin lookin for borls in the Wicar's garden, an we found a few. Thass one thing about our medder dew yew hit tew many boundaries thet dornt pay, cos yew lewse tew many borls like thet there. Still, we're found some what we lorst larst yare, so we ent got to spend no money to start this hare season orf.

Thet wor Bumble what won tha match for us larst Saturda agin them fellers from Diddlin Parva. Well, I're got to say thet wor him, hent I, cos I carnt werra well say that wor me. Mind yew, I hit tew sixes inter tha Wicar's fowl-house, but I're got to tearke my hat orf to tha way Bumble stay in an let other fellers knock em up. We allers put him in fust, cos he hully dew stop em, an thet give tha other batsmen a charnce to lash out.

Tha only time Bumble score any hisself is when he git riled. We found thet out larst yare when a silly-bold young mawther hollered out, "Come yew on, Bumble-bee, whare's yar sting?" Bumble, he went red in tha fearce, an my hart if he dint hit a six. So now we dornt say narthin till we git a bit short o' runs, an then we sharm out suffin to rile him.

We dint hatter say narthin larst Saturda, cos tha Didlin boweller riled him in tha finish. Bumble, he tarned round to pick a dandy-lion out of his crease, cos he reckoned thet wor tarnin tha borl, and while he wor bendin down tha Diddlin feller bowelled. I go to heck if thet dint ketch

Bumble a sisserara, bang plumb on tha push. Bumble jumped a yard in tha air, an let out a howl. "Thass lbw" hollered tha Diddlin captain. "Thet wornt his leg," say tha umpire. "Thet'll be yar skull in a minnit," sung out Bumble, an arter thet he hit em orl over tha shop.

Well, we won comfortable, an arterwards we drored up to the Fox for a pint apiece. Them Yanks Slim McGinty an Shorty Shultz, they watched tha match. Thet fare as if they dornt play cricket whare they come from, only rounders. "What did yew think on it?" arst Humpty Potter. "Brother," say Slim, "I'd a hed more fun settin in the church yard readin tha toom-stoons," Thass a rummun, ent it?

Harbert

TOFTREES TEARS

Fakenham's Gordon Chivers enjoyed competitive cricket for about 70 summers – and was one of a few players outside the talented Bidewell family to feature in the Toftrees line-up during the village club's golden years.

He recalled a cup game against Whissonsett on Barons Hall Lawn in Fakenham. Replying to a total of 86, Toftrees stumbled to 22 for 8. Ninth man in was mainly a bowler and he was instructed to just stop the ball and leave scoring to his partner at the other end.

An aggressive fast bowler turned a brave No 9 black and blue... but he did the job as Toftrees went on to win. And their female supporters in the crowd were so overcome with pride and emotion they all burst into tears!

On other cup-tie occasion, Toftrees were advised to take wellingtons with them for a semi-final clash at Sharrington. They found out why on arrival. The outfield had not been cut and extremely long grass made it adventurous going in the deep.

THE JOYOUS GAME

Now the joys of this game are chiefly these:
A blazing sun and a gentle breeze,
A close-cut field and shady spot
To ruminate over the runs you've got;
A clear, clean eye and a steady hand
A nerve of steel, and a cheerful band
Of fellow cricketers, one and all
Ready to welcome what'er befall.
Another to bat with, acting as one
When the moment comes for the short, sharp run;
A lithe, long bowler who gathers speed
As a Levin-bolt from a storm-cloud freed;
And a slow left-hander, subtle as sin.
A master of pitch and break and spin
A mighty hitter at number eight,
Who "lands her" over the churchyard gate;
A trusty stumper to gather them quick
And scatter the bails with a lightning flick.
The grim, set joy of a hope forlorn
When the light is bad and the pitch is worn
As you straighten your bat and face the foe,
With twenty to make and a wicket to go.'
The joy of a well-judged waiting catch
When you hug it close and settle the match;
And the ultimate joy of loser and winner'
Who fight their battles again at dinner.

A. E. Chadwick

FOURTEEN

MUSINGS AT MIKE

I took local cricket musings to the microphone on BBC Radio Norfolk in the early 1980s. Contributions to the Saturday Special sports programme tended to drift towards the light-hearted as I continued my rounds as occasional player and regular observer although I did dip into controversial waters now and again. Here are a few excerpts from scripts found mouldering at the bottom of my cricket bag.

FOUR IN A ROW

Martham legend Gerry Nichols is very useful when it comes to passing on vital information. For instance, I didn't know until he told me that a sack of coal costs more this week. Gerry should know. He sells the stuff.

But that bit of news was just in passing. What he really wants to get across is a remarkable feat performed by Martham A bowler Kevin Thornton. He collected five victims against Acle A, four of them in successive deliveries. Just to make the achievement all the more outstanding, all four were clean bowled, leg stump.

"Never heard of that before" says Gerry. "Nor has Frank High, Acle umpire standing in this match." Well, if these two can't recall such a feat in local cricket, chances are it is unique.

Kevin was presented with the match ball and the Martham lads had a reasonable excuse for a little celebration in their smart new club house... even though the match ended in a draw.

I have told Mr Nichols before but it might be worth repeating ... If he took three catches behind the stumps, thus defying those advancing years as well as the law of averages, that would go down as a Gerryatrick!

RISING DAMP

A rare old rush for cover at Lakenham on Wednesday when I popped in for chat on the first day of the Norfolk versus Hertfordshire match.

It was hot and sticky when I arrived. It was flooded out when I left. It's a bit of a job convincing people that some of us had no option but to stay put in the beer tent for over an hour while the heavens opened.

They were having fun and games in the president's tent as well, I gather, when the cress sandwiches got a bit watery and everything else fell victim to the rising damp.

Back in the beer tent, taller members of our gang had the job of pushing water over the edge from the inside as it piled up on the roof. Former Dereham player Claude Cordle mounted a chair like they do at the best parties and did his bit for the instant restoration fund with pushes in the right places.

Poor old Bill Allen, whose beloved Jentique are no more, had his shirt off before the end. And there was a fair bit of drying up to do behind the bar.

MERTON MAGIC

I'm often asked to name my favourite local cricket grounds. Well, Merton, a few miles from the metropolis of Watton, certainly deserves a place near the top of the list.

Merton Hall, home of Lord Walsingham, provides a lovely backcloth with lake close by and the world of farming all around. As the sun dips, you half expect a bell to toll in the tower and a starch-collared butler to glide down the drive with sherry on a silver salver as the string quartet tunes up and Miss Marple looks for clues.

Perhaps that's just me or anyone else trapped quite happily in the web of nostalgia woven round the golden era of country house cricket and England, Their England.

I hope the action continues at Merton for as long as the old game is played. But I know the club have the sort of worries so familiar to many in the area. The Watton revival under Andy Agar, with big plans for the future including a second team, is bound to attract more talent from surrounding villages like Saham Toney and Merton.

I'm not knocking the idea of some youngsters moving on to bigger clubs. That's part and parcel of our scene these days. But "heritage" and "loyalty" are not dirty words in my scorebook either.

Talking of devotion to certain clubs, let me take my hat off to the likes of Monty Montague, tireless worker on and off the field for Thorpe-based St Andrews, Ron Dobbie, Aldborough's amiable work-horse, and evergreen Tony Curson, who does so much for Hethersett.

Tony sets a teasing example to youngsters who are told not be ashamed to spin the ball and pitch it up. Will that Curson delivery ever get there? Plenty of chances at Hethersett for all sorts of players, young and old, with a fixture card stretching to over 60 outings.

Perhaps only Aldborough fit in more. But they do try to get the season over by Christmas.

HIRED GUNS?

No doubt about this weekend's big match – the Bob Carter Cup final

Aldborough stalwart Ron Dobbie reaches 70 not out - with his beloved village green behind him. In all he filled a series of committee and playing posts at the club over more than sixty years. He claimed over 3000 wickets and took over 100 wickets in a season 14 times - testament to traditional virtues of line and length.

at Lakenham between Ingham and Dereham. And if you weigh up Ingham's chances in cup competitions these days, you're bound to pass more than a cursory glance in the direction of Parvez Mir, the gifted Pakistani putting his talents on show for both Ingham and Norfolk this season.

His presence at club level has added more fuel to the fire stoked up by Norwich club Barleycorns when they put out the welcome mat for Australians and New Zealanders, and Cavaliers when Kiwi Ross Ormiston renewed his links with local action as he turned out for them last season in big matches.

Carter Cup rules do not specify that such players must not turn out in the Sunday ties, but you can't help wondering if the whole thing won't escalate to unmanageable proportions in the next couple of seasons if it isn't checked.

It can be argued that Ingham are good enough to win trophies without Parvez Mir – they did it last year – but his personal contributions in the last few months underline just what an influence he can exert at this level.

Is that the thin end of the wedge? Will other clubs say "Right, if that's the game let's hit the road and hire a couple of big boys for next season."

Let's not be hypocritical about this. Ingham were heard to utter the odd complaint about Barleycorns' talented imports, so they should have been ready for this summer's words of criticism on the balmy air.

I don't want to over-dramatise and call them "hired guns". I know how the system works – and indeed seems to have been fully accepted – in the Minor Counties. However, the general verdict must be that it goes against the spirit of the Bob Carter competition, set in motion for senior Norfolk clubs in 1969.

And you have to ask what damage can be done to a club's morale when loyal servants have to stand aside for Mister Big. Have you been a victim of that? How did you react? Is it nice to hear your club called a load of pot-hunters?

And when Mister Big's packed his bags and gone somewhere else, how do you feel when they say "Can you turn out for us this week?"

I know where I'd tell them to stick their selection sheet.

Determination from Cromer's Phil Mindham in a Carter Cup tie.

HUMBLE PIE

I have received a menacing letter from Valerie Farrow who writes (bread knife in hand) on behalf of a certain contingent at Norwich club Mallards and any others who feel like cutting up rough.....

"Spare a thought for the most important members of the cricket scene who were left out when you extolled the joys of the game and signs of the coming season.

"Week after week these stalwarts prepare themselves for the onslaught of 22 good men and true and for a brief 20-minute innings face all that a good team can deliver!

"I refer, of course, to the backbone of any good club, ladies of the tea rota. Unlike a current commercial, they rarely receive a box of chocolates and soldier on throughout the season up to their eyes in sliced bread and sponge cake.

"Please, Keith, give them a plug. Cricket tea ladies of the world, unite!"

Valerie, I am ready for a portion of humble pie. And chocolates are in the post.

ROYAL VICTIM

Charles Wright, a Dereham solicitor who died in 1886, was an outstanding cricketer in his day and played for Norfolk.

He was specially celebrated as a bowler and a story is told that he once bowled King Edward VII, when Prince of Wales, first ball.

The incident was severely criticised at the time and it was said he should have given HRH a chance by sending up an easy one.

THE GAME THAT'S NEVER DONE

Soft, soft the sunset falls upon the pitch,
The game is over and the stumps are drawn,
The willow sleeps in it appointed niche,
The heavy roller waits another dawn –
Bowled is the final ball again,
Hushed is the umpires' call again,
The fielders and the batsmen cease to run –
But memory will play again
Many and many a day again
The game that's done, the game that's never done.

In happy dreams we'll see each ball re-bowled,
And mend the fault that robbed us of some prize,
In dreams we'll hold the catch we failed to hold,
And see our duck's-eggs swell to centuries –
In dreams we'll take the field again,
In dreams the willow wield again,
And set the red ball spinning in the sun –
Ah, memory will play again
Many and many a day again
The game that's done, the game that's never done.

Eleanor and Herbert Farjeon

JUST A MINUTE

A couple of items from Narborough Cricket Club's minute books extracted by David Turner:

February 16th, 1933- "it was unamiously (sic) carried that all members of the team pay 9d each so as to cover all expenses."

August 3rd, 1948 – "Fund-raising fete; Swaffham Town Band was to be engaged to supply the music, if not too expensive. Otherwise an Electric Reproducer was to be found."

FIFTEEN

POLLY WIGGLE'S TEST

Time for a test set by the county's most famous tea-lady, the redoubtable Polly Wiggle. She has the perfect answer to keep the boys amused should rain stop play. How many of the 31 Norfolk place names can you find? Polly does take one or two liberties – but she has to make it quite difficult with one of her famous strawberry flans as top prize!

Picture, if you will, a summer field, daisies growing in abundance around the boundary, a close-cropped wicket cut right in the centre, under the crowning glory of a blue summer sky, with only the tiniest hint of the rainclouds that are forecast for the afternoon.

Village cricket captain Stan Ford steps out towards the pavilion which, to be kind, has seen better days. He stops, wipes his shoe on the grass. "I see someone left the dam' gate open again" he mutters "hope they cleared the rest o' the field". Fishing in his pocket he produces a set of keys and selects the rustiest, fitting it to the equally rusty lock. Gently forcing the stiff key to turn he opens the doors wide, releasing the fusty air caused by damp and months of under-use of the building. The first match of the season is soon to be under way.

Gradually the rest of the team arrive and the building warms with relatively good-natured banter. Jim Sutton and Mike Thompson arrive together, as they have for every match anyone can remember, closely followed by vice captain Ian Massingham and Tim Worth. Cousins Clint and David Green, for some obscure reason nicknamed Caffy and Daffy, have yet again settled their differences and shared a lift to the ground with Jo Thorpe and the new boy Brad Well. Peter Middleton roars up on his motorbike, apologising for the row as he tumbles into the pavilion, explaining "M' car brook down again – hed ter git th' ole bike out!" Naturally, Croft is last to arrive, he'll be here soon.

The changing room floor is soon littered with kit as everyone starts changing for the game. Croft arrives, in a hurry as usual and blunders in. Stopping just in time he calls out: "Shift that bag, Thorpe, I nearly broke my neck over it!" Some wag calls out: "That's a bit over the top, Croft! If you can't see that bag you shouldn't be playing cricket." Thorpe's bag is enormous and the source of endless ribbing for the unfortunate owner.

Soon everyone's changed and moving to the outfield for a bit of practice, greeting the tea ladies on the way out. Mrs Ford (ham sandwiches), Ivy Todd (sponge cakes and occasionally Eccles cakes), and Ethel Mayes (jam tarts to die for) are all well-known.

Sam Todd, Ivy's husband, known to all as Stoddy since he signs everything he can lay his hands on "S Todd", sharpens his pencil and arranges his seat to be able to see the umpires. He lists the team in the score book before informing Stan "Thass dun'um".

Stan, meanwhile, is searching high and low, gradually getting crosser and crosser. Nearly seething, he finally shouts "Has anyone seen the other dam' bail – I've got three and can't find the other! It's nowhere to be seen." A concerted effort by tea ladies, scorer and one or two members of the opposition reveal the offending article, lurking in the corner where it had rolled. "Thank you, Hethel" murmurs Stan, trying to be polite.

Practise is going well. Croft is making Worth move to catch the ball, suggesting it's "'bowt time yew ran, Worth! Yew dunt dew much on the pitch!" Sutton skies one following an early-season wayward ball from Caffy, while Daffy remarks: "Cor, blarst, that went up well!"

His temper restored having passed the wickets and all four bails to the umpires, Stan calls a team talk. "Now, lads, we hent played this lot a'fore, so I suggest we start slowly. Sutton and Massingham will open the bowling. Young Brad, field in the slips to start, I'll perhaps bring you on to bowl later. Croft, go out well beyond square leg, you've got a strong arm to throw back in. The rest of you I'll place when we see how things go.

A quick glance to see all was ready and the toss is made. Stan chooses to field first so out go the team, the opposition joining wives and family on the boundary. One dad is immediately grabbed by a youngster to play horsey while he is waiting to bat, another sits himself comfortably down, being last man in, and gently dozes, soon mildly snoring.

The opposition openers, Will Westwick and Percy Blakeney walk to the crease and the gentle thud of leather on willow announces the start of another season.

NORFOLK LOCATIONS:

Summerfield • Stanford • Damgate • Stiffkey
Sutton • Thompson • Massingham • Clint Green • Daffy Green
Thorpe • Bradwell • Middleton • Carbrooke • Bagthorpe
Topcroft Fordham • Ivy Todd • Stody! • Dunham! • Bale!
Nowhere • Hethel • Ranworth • Upwell • Sloley! • Bradfield
Outwell • Horsey • Snoring • Westwick • Blakeney

SIXTEEN

CLOSE OF PLAY

On the green they watched their sons

Playing till too dark to see,

As their fathers watched them once,

As my father once watched me,

While the bat and beetle flew

On the warm air webbed with dew.

Edmund Blunden

TIME TO GO

The *Eastern Daily Press* carried the following on Monday, September 11th, 1893:

In a village match in Kent an umpire had three times refused to say "Out" when a batsman, hitting hard against time, was palpably stumped

The wicketkeeper in despair, having again appealed in vain, seized and shouldered the middle stump and, in spite of protests, marched up and down the wicket like one demented.

At length the umpire, seeing that time was precious, approached the batsman and said;" I think you had better go, sir."

And he went.